Douglas Scott

JONATHAN GLANCEY

The Design Council

First published 1988 in the United Kingdom by
The Design Council
28 Haymarket
London SW1Y 4SU

Typeset by Colset Private Ltd, Singapore

Printed by Jolly & Barber Ltd, Rugby

British Library Cataloguing in Publication Data
Glancey, Jonathan
    Douglas Scott.
    1. Scott, Douglas, 1913- 2. Industrial
    designers—Great Britain—Biography
    I. Title
    745.2′092′4   TS140.S3/

ISBN 0 85072 215 2

Contents

UNIVERSAL LENS-CRAFT

Chronology

Dates of products refer to the year of design and not necessarily to the date of manufacture.

1913	Born Kennington, London.
1926–29	Central School of Arts and Crafts, trains as silversmith.
1929–33	Lighting designer with Osler & Faraday, Birmingham.
1933–36	Lighting designer with GVD Illuminators, London.
1936–39	Industrial designer in Raymond Loewy Studio, London:

	1938	Aga cooker redesign, Allied Ironfounders
	1938	Rayburn cooker, Allied Ironfounders
	1937–9	Domestic equipment, GEC
	1938–9	Street lighting, GEC
	1939	Avery weighing machine
	1939	Hillman Minx prototypes, Rootes

1939–45	Test, repair and development work on aero engines, De Havilland, Hendon.
1945	Sets up evening industrial design course at Central School.
1945–49	Freelance designer:

1945 Ship's binnacle, Henry Hughes & Son
1946 RTC double-deck coach, London Transport
1947 Luggage, Papworth Industries
1947 Pens, packaging, desk-top accessories, Eternor
1948 Radio cabinet and relay set, Rediffusion
1948 RF Coach, London Transport

1946	Teaches industrial design course full time at Central School.
1949	Resigns from Central School.
1949–55	Scott–Ashford Associates:

1949 RF single-deck bus, London Transport
1952 Clocks, Westclox
1953 Routemaster double-deck bus, London Transport
1954 Canteen seating, London Transport
1955 Lorry cab, AEC

1952–76	Resumes part-time teaching, as senior lecturer, at Central School.
1955–76	DS/Douglas Scott Associates:

1957 Tape deck, British Sound Recorders
1958 MY *Tamarind*
1962 STD public telephone, GPO

1963 Farlander collapsible caravan, Compton Co
1964 Roma bathroom suite, Ideal-Standard
1965 Mk V zoom lens TV camera, Marconi
1966 Prototype telephone kiosk, GPO
1966 Mobile dockside crane, N C K Rapier Ltd
1967 Hy-Mac Excavator, Peter Hamilton Ltd
1968 System Four Computer, English Electric
1970 Mk VIII colour TV camera, Marconi

1974   Royal Designer for Industry.

1976–79   Professor of Industrial Design, Universidad Nacional Autonoma de Mexico.

1979   Freelance lecturer and design consultant.

1985   Japan Design Foundation Award, Osaka.

LONDON BUSES LTD

Pre-prototype model in Plasticine, scale 1:5, of the Routemaster bus, 1952.

Douglas Scott

Preface

I first met Douglas Scott in 1985, but like countless thousands of people throughout the world, had, often unwittingly, been very familiar with his work since childhood. Until recently I did not know that he had designed such classics as London Transport's Routemaster bus, and Ideal – Standard's Roma wash-basin found throughout the world as well as in the Museum of Modern Art in New York. Scott's work is easily taken for granted because it is assimilated so naturally into our everyday lives.

Scott is a retiring man who shies away from publicity. He was unsure of having any sort of book written about him, but agreed that if there had to be one (there did), then it should be a record of his working life and not a colourful biography. So here it is, a book that I hope is a fair and commonsensical appraisal of 50 years in the life of a hard-working designer. Scott would put most of his designs down to teamwork, but his contribution to the products he has worked on has always been quietly dominant, mostly because he has always made a particular effort to understand materials and production processes as well as clients' and consumers' desires.

The book was suggested to the Design Council by Dinah Casson and commissioned by Jony Russell. Stephanie Horner has more than patiently seen it through to publication. My thanks to these three and to Douglas and Kathy Scott for their hospitality, patience and practical wisdom.

Thanks must also go to the Benedictine community of St Augustine's Abbey, Ramsgate, who provided a week's peace and quiet to draft the manuscript.

Jonathan Glancey
Ramsgate, May 1987

Mk Ia Spitfire, 1940. Original design by William Mitchell for Supermarine.

ROYAL AERONAUTICAL SOCIETY

Mk II Jaguar, 1959. Design by William Lyons.

NATIONAL MOTOR MUSEUM. BEAULIEU

Introduction

As a designer Douglas Scott stands as much on the side of the machine toolist and production engineer as he does of the advertising agency, salesman and consumer. His approach to design has been practical, unselfconscious, behind the scenes and very British. He has worked to improve the design and performance of machines that, unglamorous though they might be, are the basic props of our everyday world from switchgear and transmitters to boilers and tin-openers. The most banal object becomes elegant in the hands of a designer concerned as much with usefulness, durability and maintenance as with style.

If Scott had been born thirty years earlier, he might well have been apprenticed to one of the great railway engineering workshops, producing the kind of restrained and natural design solutions that led gradually to the supremely elegant British steam locomotives of Nigel Gresley, Charles Collett or William Stanier. The young engineering draughtsmen who styled these machines remain anonymous and forgotten figures. But Scott has lived into the age of the designer as media star and pop personality, a phenomenon he mistrusts.

It is a characteristic of much great British design up until the mid-twentieth century that the author of a particular product or machine is unknown or overlooked. Only very recently has Scott's name been attached to London Transport's famous Routemaster bus (on which he worked with the LT engineer Eric Ottoway and his team at Chiswick Bus Works), and yet

Classic flowing lines of an LNER Gresley A3 Pacific (built from 1927), distinctive under British Railway's grime 35 years on.

anyone looking carefully at this elegant vehicle knows instinctively that a guiding hand has been at work, softening its focus, endowing a massive public service vehicle with graceful curves and civic manners.

But if many classic British designs were the work of engineers with an intuitive sense of form and style – Mitchell's Spitfire, William Lyons's Mk II Jaguar (1959), Nigel Gresley's A3 Pacific (1927) – this was due partly at least to the simple fact that the industrial designer was an unknown quantity until the late 1930s. Douglas Scott was one of Britain's first professional industrial designers. Entering a world dominated by engineers he has always respected their part in the manufacturing process. Despite being a protégé of a new, glamorous and much-hyped profession, Scott has never been scornful of the anonymous engineering tradition in British design.

In fact professional designers and architects (who feel they can design anything) have blundered badly where engineers have triumphed. Ludwig Mies van der Rohe's attempt, for example, to design a car body for the Adler (1931) was a distinct failure. The architect who designed the revolutionary and beautiful Barcelona Pavilion (1929) produced a bulbous, retrograde car. Frank Pick's gifted architect, Charles Holden, responsible for Arnos Grove (1932) and Southgate Underground stations (1933–34) failed dismally when he turned his hand to designing a double deck bus. In the 1950s and 60s Jaguar looked on as several famous Italian designers took a fresh look at the sensational E-type Jaguar. Michelotti, Bertone and 'Pinin' Farina all failed to match the sensational and convincing lines of Jaguar's own bodywork, styled in Coventry by the racing engineer Malcolm Sayer and William Lyons.

So when Scott joined Raymond Loewy's new London office in 1936, he found more to admire in the practical approach to product design of the flamboyant American's number two, Carl Otto, who had served his time in the workshops of General Motors in Detroit, than in the brilliant self-publicist who employed him. Scott believes that it is no use being asked to style a product unless you know exactly how that

Greyhound bus. Design by Raymond Loewy.

MCDONNELL DOUGLAS

Douglas DC3, 1935, by McDonnell Douglas Corporation.

ALTOONA AREA PUBLIC LIBRARY

Steam locomotive. Design by Raymond Loewy.

product is made, how it will work and how long it will last. If the designer has a proven grounding in machine tooling and production engineering then it becomes possible to make changes to a product. If a designer can suggest new methods of production and can design the tools required for production, then the nature and looks of a product can be changed radically. For Scott, designers walk naked when applying a mere surface gloss.

Designed from first principles, from tooling to marketing strategies, a product tends to be long-lived, with the initial investment being repaid many times over through a long sales life. Scott has proved time and again that a well thought out product will sell for years. It should also last for years. His designs in the public sector have been extraordinarily durable: this list includes the standard General Post Office (GPO) pay-phone of the 1960s (20 years; replaced by new technology); the low-cost Roma wash-basin for Ideal-Standard designed in 1964 and still selling in vast quantities world wide; the London Transport single deck RF bus (in service from 1951 to 1976); the Routemaster double deck bus (in service since 1959 and still good enough, according to London Transport engineers, to run into the next century). There are 35 year-old Scott-designed street lamps in Sydney, while thousands of kitchens across Europe and the USA clatter to the sound of Scott's Prestige kitchen equipment. Behind the scenes in public buildings and corporate headquarters the world over there are countless boilers, controls and transmitters that have benefited from his fundamental approach to design.

What Scott has never had is a public persona. Certainly he has won awards, including the coveted RDI (Royal Designer for Industry), but he has shied away from self-promotion. Perhaps he has simply been too busy to court publicity. He was criticised by academics for his teaching style at the Central School of Art in the late 1940s. He was, they said, too matter of fact. Reported by school inspectors to the Ministry of Education for his practical approach to design education, he was encouraged to resign. In setting students real design projects, by insisting they understood and stuck to cost limits and by asking them to make what they had designed, Scott was attempting to ease the transition from theory to practice. Perhaps terse discussions about tooling, machining, production processes, costs of materials and so on can prove boring to aspiring young designers, media-struck and obsessed with style alone, but he insisted on driving the message home that a lack of understanding of machining and tooling would cripple Britain's post-war industrial effort. It did.

Scott's training as a craftsman gave him an intrinsic understanding and feeling for materials. During his days as a student at the Central School of Arts and Crafts he spent many laborious hours filing to obtain perfectly smooth surfaces. He got to know the properties, characteristics and limits of a wide range of materials. The craft process also meant that he had to design in three dimensions from the outset. Since his days at the Central, Scott has never enjoyed designing isolated parts of a product on a drawing board – a dashboard, for example, for a Hillman or a rear light cluster for a Sunbeam (both jobs he undertook during his spell at Loewy's). He has always liked to get a grasp on a complete project and see it through from blueprint to working prototype.

Although he has worked for a large number of bureaucratic organisations, Scott has tried to avoid design by committee. He believes that this approach is a recipe for disaster and cites the British car industry as an example of what can go wrong. In designing the Routemaster bus for London Transport he worked alone with a small team of four or five engineers. On any matter concerning the design of the bodywork or interior, he would be called to Chiswick before the project moved to the next stage of development.

The immediate and enduring success of the Routemaster bus lay partly in rigorous testing and partly in its gradual introduction into service. The prototype ran for five years from 1954 until mass production began in 1959. By the time the bus was put into everyday service it was as reliable as it was ever going to be. Yet, despite pleas by Scott among others, this was a lesson from which British industry was not keen to learn in the 1950s and 60s. When, for example, Rootes rushed its new Hillman Imp into production amid a blaze of publicity in 1962, the car was beset with teething problems that were not ironed out until thousands of customers had suffered. In some ways superior to the Issigonis-designed British Motor Corporation Mini (engine, transmission, quality of ride), its immediate rival, the Imp, which had promised thousands of new jobs in Scotland, found favour with an ever-decreasing proportion of the car-buying public. Customers wanted a production vehicle, not a rolling test bed.

This sad story was repeated many times over by other British manufacturers in both the private and commercial sectors. Small wonder that tried and tested foreign cars and lorries began appearing on British streets in ever-increasing numbers from the mid-1960s onwards.

But in all his concern for sound engineering and methods of production, Scott has never lost sight of what makes a product good-looking. His best designs are characterised by a subtle use of curving surfaces – Hogarth's bounding curve and a feature of the finest British product design from shoes to Spitfires. Scott says that he learned the curve from Loewy; before then he was designing neo-classical lamp fittings for traditionalist architects, Edwin Lutyens and Herbert Baker among them, which gave him little opportunity to develop a line in flowing curves. Loewy's use of the bounding line was often gloriously exaggerated, unlike the long tradition of subtle curves in British design before the streamline era. Where the love of this form comes from is difficult to say. Perhaps the gently undulating British countryside has something to do with it; perhaps there is a deep-rooted mistrust of hard Germanic edges; perhaps the contemplation of the racehorse has even more to do with it. But, whatever its origin, the curving line has graced countless British machines that would have seemed stark and brutal without them. Scott designed the Routemaster bus with so many curves to create, first, a reduction in visual bulk and second, a seamless sequence of surfaces. As a result the bus was easy on the eye and, displaying Scott's practical nature once again, very easy to clean.

But Scott also says that the straight line demands perfect workmanship. Imperfections show all too obviously on a poorly worked flat surface.

Scott's work has been accused of lacking in warmth. This is obviously not true of the early work – radio-receiver cabinets, for instance, which were made in rich wood veneers – but is presumably levelled at the vast range of control gear, computer equipment and domestic boilers he produced during the 1960s and 70s. Certainly there is a current vogue for brightening up equipment, but most backroom machinery, especially if it is to last many years, needs to be quietly designed, well ordered, common-sensical, easy to use and maintain. In the 1980s there has been a lot of talk about the need for products to satisfy emotional needs, but there are limits. New fridges with pedimented tops are a lot of fun in magazine articles and exhibitions, but how much character do you need to give your fridge? Does the addition of a pretty roof rob small kitchens of much needed storage space? Do the highly articulated panels make it difficult to clean?

Scott has spent a large part of his career taming control gear that had been put together in an *ad hoc* fashion, which has made life easier and faster for the electrician, but more or less impossible for the operator. During the 1950s and 60s – before transistors and silicon chips – much control gear was in danger of being strangled by yards of wire and cable and cluttered up with switches, dials and levers. To organise control panels in an orderly fashion and to stow cables away in neat lockers was a godsend for those who had to use them. One of the great luxuries of computer control is that information can be presented digitally in small displays so gone are the impressive rows of dials and switches found, for example, in Scott's building control room in the basement of the Shell Centre. Computer screens can be housed in any shape or form the buyer wants, be it a neat black box or a plastic model of Daffy Duck.

What Scott was doing in his design of clinical-looking backroom control systems was bringing order to the chaos of pre-computer electronics. In the 1980s there is far more room for manoeuvre.

Nevertheless, Scott's designs in this period were notably hygienic. The small domestic wall-mounted boiler for Potterton, for example, which sold in countless thousands, is about as simple and clean cut a container as you could get outside, or indeed inside, a laboratory. Should domestic machinery be more colourful and richer in form and texture?

During the consumer boom dating from the late 1950s onwards many British buyers were getting a first opportunity to buy domestic hardware and gadgetry that was new and clean. The vast majority of the population cooked and cleaned in small bitty kitchens, cluttered with a mish-mash of machinery dominated by an old cast-iron horseshoe boiler that needed constant feeding to provide hot water. The new ranges of sinks, cookers, fridges, gadgetry and boilers offered by companies like Potterton, Ideal-Standard and Prestige and designed by Douglas Scott among others were just what they dreamed of. The age of coal dust, soot and smog was on the wane – the new arctic domestic landscape was a reflection of people's wish for a clean start.

Inevitably the pendulum has begun to swing the other way and now that the majority of the population lives in reasonably hygienic-looking conditions there is a desire to break out of this hospital-like aesthetic and return to warmth, decoration and colour.

But how obsessive a consumer do you have to be to want a carpet-sweeper more complex in form than Scott's Ewbank model for Prestige? Should an icing gun be as elaborate as the frothy decoration it helps create? Do you really want your kettle to be the major talking-point over supper?

When you look at things the other way round you quickly discover that restrained designers like Douglas Scott have brought great harmony and beauty to commonplace objects used by everyone, which need a degree of moderation – a calming touch. As in his two greatest designs – the Routemaster bus and the basin for Ideal Standard – he brought a very sophisticated approach to design down from Parnassus to the market-place. You may not stop very often to contemplate the Ideal-Standard wash-basin, and its beauty of line may not be brought home to you until you see it prominently displayed in an art museum and labelled as a classic of modern design. Similarly your appreciation of a Routemaster bus might well be linked directly to the number of minutes you have to wait for one on the way to work – again opinions would change if the 7.25 ton (7.3 tonne) bus were polished up and put in a museum. Most critics have something good to say about the Routemaster now that it is disappearing. During the run of its 30-year life they have abstained from comment – a not quite silent servant (the gargle of the 9.6-litre diesel is as familiar a sound in London as the FXR4/5 taxi, as under-rated as its designer).

Douglas Scott has not been a revolutionary designer. His work has often been a sober reappraisal of imperfectly realised products. An unselfconscious designer, he nevertheless has a shrewd idea of what appeals to a mass market over a number of years. His strength as a designer – aside from his understanding of tools, production engineering and cost – is his ability to create a product in the consumer market that is not only credible but taken for granted 10 or 20 years after it is put on sale.

When asked what the favourite among his designs was the prolific Italian designer Achille Castiglioni chose without hesitation a small light-switch, an inconspicuous but perfectly realised object which has sold in millions. Castiglioni – although a man who designs for the fashion market – takes a quiet pleasure in the fact that wherever he stays he finds the light-switch he designed. Scott gets the same quiet satisfaction from seeing street lamps he designed 40 years ago, buses of 30 years ago, and bathroom equipment of 20 years ago still in use. Yet Scott is not affected by undue nostalgia. If the lamps, buses or basins were outmoded and being kept for purely sentimental reasons, as a designer he would find that galling. His career has been dedicated to efficient engineering and designing order out of engineering chaos, resulting in very practical styling.

The danger as Scott sees it is of designers being too fashion conscious and their work being seen as ephemera. The ironic work produced by Milanese designers between 1979 and 1985 already seems gloriously anachronistic.

No matter how unfashionable his work might seem today, Douglas Scott's designs will endure. He will be remembered as one of the quiet masters of practical styling.

Above: *Art nouveau silver (1907) designed by Augustus Steward, Head of Metalwork at the Central School of Art. Scott was one of his students.*
Below: *Fanciful silver cups by Augustus Steward, c. 1907.*

Chapter 1
Early Days

Douglas Scott says that he is a designer by accident. He always wanted to be a writer. As a boy he devoured poetry and short stories, but harsh economic realities pushed him away from literature and into handicraft. In a sense he was following or being guided along his father's footsteps. Scott senior came from a family of Perthshire wine merchants. The only boy among nine children, his career got off to a promising start when he was articled to a solicitor. But when his father died suddenly at an early age, the articles vanished and with them the lucrative future career they had promised.

Douglas Scott's father trained instead as an electrician. Although a literary young man, a skill in a booming trade guaranteed a secure living. Concerned that his own son should not want for money, Scott senior encouraged Douglas to take up metalwork at the Central School of Arts and Crafts when he was 13 with a London County Council three-year scholarship.

If his father encouraged the cautious, practical side of Scott's nature, his mother's family helped create the teacher. They had been farmers in Scotland, but her father had turned to antique furniture restoration and dealing. Her mother was a religious zealot who lectured in classic Bible-thumping style. There is something of the missionary in Douglas Scott's career as a teacher of design, but that is a much later story.

Douglas Scott was born on 4 April 1913 in Kennington, South London. His earliest memories are of sheltering in the local police station during night-time air raids. His uncle's drum factory nearby was destroyed. But there were other less terrifying distractions. The circus came regularly to the Kennington Theatre and the gentler animals like the camels would be housed in the stables belonging to the corner dairy. Other diversions included visits to his father's cousin's saddlery in the Strand, near Waterloo Bridge.

Scott attended the local junior church school – St Philip's, Lambeth, where he excelled in English and spelling – before moving on to the Archbishop Temple's School, Lambeth, a grammar school dating back to Cromwell's time, which thrived on hard work. The boys worked on Saturdays, discipline was rigid and positions in class were given every week. The school produced a large number of journalists and stockbrokers, but was not particularly concerned with the arts. But, as Scott recalls, he was 'quite shocking at woodwork and hopeless at technical drawing'. He felt he had no natural talent whatsoever at the time. But what he had learnt from family and school was a sense of propriety, self-discipline and common sense, qualities that were to stand him in good stead when he worked with flamboyant designers in later years.

When Scott arrived at the Central School in 1926 the Department of Metal Studies was at its peak under the vigorous Augustus Steward. Scott, training as a silversmith, recalls that the teachers were good craftsmen who really cared about their young pupils. 'We were forced to be good', Scott recalls. He became something of an expert in soldering.

But even the best possible training as a silversmith at the time of the Great Depression was no guarantee of a secure future. Some students went into journalism; others became dealers. Scott felt he was lucky to land a job as a 'general dogsbody' in the design studio of the long-established electric light company Osler and Faraday, based in Birmingham. Fred Burrage, the etcher, was then Principal of the Central School and recommended the 16-year-old Scott to a friend, Herbert Pepper, who was then Chief Designer at Osler and Faraday. Scott jumped at the chance. Although it could hardly be described as the most glamorous job in the world, the company offered to pay him 25 shillings (£1.25) a week, twice as much as an average apprentice.

Osler and Faraday was an old-fashioned, craft-based company. It produced mostly period-style electric light fittings at its works in Broad Street, Birmingham and sold them at home and abroad. The company was particularly successful in India. It could boast fittings in Buckingham Palace and the Palace of Westminister. Osler had set out manufacturing glass fittings (dolls' eyes in particular) and had shown crystal cut glass chandeliers at the Great Exhibition of 1851.

Although most of Osler and Faraday's fittings were very traditional, Scott found it an excellent place to train. The workmanship was of the very highest order. Scott's drawings were watercolours on tinted paper which would be shown to the grand architects who visited the works to arrange custom-made fittings for their latest project. Edwin Lutyens and Herbert Baker specified electric light fittings from Osler's for their imperial buildings in New Delhi.

Osler and Faraday found Scott to be a willing and useful assistant. Unlike some of the ex-art students they had taken on, his practical approach to design was invaluable. He was sent on a six-month tour of Britain's booming cinemas, producing designs for neo-Greek and art deco fittings. Scott had certainly heard of the Bauhaus, but its impact on Britain was still minimal. While Marcel Breuer was designing his purist globe lamps, Scott was designing Grecian pendants for Wimbledon Town Hall. In 1932 he was moved to Birmingham to work on reducing costs of custom-designed fittings by using existing castings and choosing assembly methods and parts which lowered costs without affecting the appearance.

Scott moved back to London in 1933, taking on a job as Chief Designer at the small lighting firm GVD Illuminators. He was paid £5 a week, which was good money for a 20-year-old. At GVD Scott worked with architects in designing shadow-free illumination for rooms. Concealed lighting was coming into vogue and Scott, who had spent four years at Osler and Faraday designing bold, decorative fittings, was now having to hide his light behind a cornice. But he spent a useful three years with the company, during which time he began attending night school at the Willesden College of Art where he eventually gained a Diploma in Industrial Design.

Industrial design was a new concept in Britain at that time. Until the emergence of a self-conscious industrial design profession in the 1930s, products were the work of anonymous draughtsmen, craftsmen and engineers. Occasionally a well-known architect or artist might try his hand, but there were no professional industrial designers. But, unknown to Douglas Scott, while he was working as a lighting designer for GVD a practice of industrial designers had moved into premises in the same building, three floors above him in Aldwych House. This outfit was the London branch of Raymond Loewy Associates. Loewy was the already very successful American designer, showman and marketeer who employed an English designer – John Beresford Evans. Just as the London office needed to take on another homespun designer, Douglas Scott had reached the point at GVD where 'if I designed another light fitting, I'd develop an attack of the screaming abdabs!' He was spared that bizarre fate and instead became one of Britain's first professional industrial designers.

Presentation sketch of pendant lamp for Wimbledon Town Hall. Osler & Faraday, c. 1932.

THE DESIGN MUSEUM

Raymond Loewy flanked by Studebaker Champion and streamlined S1 locomotive, 1939.

Chapter 2
The Loewy Studio 1936–39

On the fifth floor of Aldwych House Raymond Loewy had set up his new London design studio. All Douglas Scott had to do to get a job was to climb three flights of stairs, talk things over with Carl Otto (an automotive engineer and stylist who had previously worked in the USA for General Motors and the visionary designer Norman Bel-Geddes) and sign on the dotted line. 'When can you start?', Otto demanded, offering an astonished Scott £8 a week. This was in November 1936 when the best paid manual workers were earning less than half that sum.

The office was tiny but beautifully decorated in an International Modern idiom – white walls, lightweight furniture by Ludwig Mies van der Rohe and Marcel Breuer, blue and grey linoleum floors, pale blue carpets and large blown-up black and white photographs mounted in slim white frames. 'It didn't look like a work place', Scott says. Carl Otto ran the office taking care of the business end. Scott joined Beresford Evans as a designer. Loewy himself would keep in touch by telephone but only visited occasionally.

Work generated and designed in London was very much a local affair. Loewy had other, bigger fish to fry in the United States, but one of the London office's big breaks came when Loewy visited the office in the summer of 1937. The Aldwych House office had been given to Loewy by Sigmund Gestetner – of office equipment fame – who introduced Loewy in London to Rootes, the motor manufacturer. This gave Scott and Beresford Evans the chance to work on a Plasticine mock-up of a new 3-litre Sunbeam Talbot design for a sports car. Scott remembers Lord Rootes showing a visitor the interior of the Plasticine prototype and in his enthusiasm putting his foot on and destroying the running board.

Despite this incident, Plasticine remained a key tool in the Loewy design studio. It could be sculpted precisely and finished with a high polish. Models of the prototype 1939 Hillman Minx show how working with Plasticine allowed the designers to make subtle changes to designs they were unsure of. The Minx models were made at 1:8 scale, but the Sunbeam Talbot was life-size and – as Lord Rootes proved – very lifelike.

Although work at Loewy's was fun – it was a sociable, high-spirited, noisy office – it was also exceptionally hard. Scott was living at home in Kingsbury at the time and would get the workman's train into town in the mornings. Midnight marked the end of a typical working day, but Scott often found himself toiling away all night. Sunday was more often than not a day off. When he did try to take a two-week holiday in Denmark he was summoned back to the office three days earlier than planned.

Quite simply there was a lot of work to be done. The Loewy office was unique in Britain. Wells Coates, a practising architect, designed some notable radio sets for Ekco, but he had no industrial design experience as such. Loewy's practice was the only purely professional industrial design office in the country. Carl Otto was out of the office most of the week drumming up business, which was probably a good thing. Dynamic and bursting with ideas, Otto's temper was notoriously volatile. The times he hurled his telephone across the room were too numerous to count. His language was a mixture of drawling sophisticated American and a spray of abusive Anglo-Saxon. Any lulls in the office were spent in heavy political rows (Scott was fairly left wing) or discussing the periodicals Loewy would send over from the States. Scott was now eagerly devouring anything on new product design and was certainly at this stage influenced by

American streamlining. His first solo design for Loewy was a streamlined flat iron, transforming an object of household drudgery into a stylish piece of kitchen equipment.

Scott's down-to-earth common sense complemented Beresford Evans's intellectual Bauhaus approach to design. As the practice expanded, the peripatetic Carl Otto would whisk expensive-looking American businessmen into and out of the office. The American influence was considerable despite the independent status of the studio. When the Loewy team designed a new radio for Philco it was panned by the influential *Architectural Review* for looking too much like a General Motors' radiator grille. But with a retail price of six guineas (£6.30), the buying public saw it as style within reach.

The Loewy office in London closed in 1939, undermined by the advent of the Second World War. But in that short period it had built up an impressive roll of clients – General Electric Company (GEC), Allied Ironfounders, Rootes and Electrolux among them. Scott was particularly proud of his 1938 redesign of the Aga

Teabreak in the Loewy office. Left to right: Ursula Staples-Smith, who was Carl Otto's secretary; Bill Snaith's assistant – a quiet English architect, only ever known as Dixie; and Scott's assistant, Carl Neilssen.

stove for Allied Ironfounders. This gave the ungainly but efficient cooker a new lease of life that lasted the next forty years. Scott went on to design the Rayburn cooker in 1938, also for Allied Ironfounders. For Electrolux he collaborated on the design of refrigerators and vacuum cleaners – domestic objects transformed out of all recognition during this period.

Scott was learning a considerable amount about slick packaging – or styling – in this period. Some would argue that packaging was the sum of Loewy's achievement. But styling was more important than purists could ever admit. Goods had to sell and there is no doubt that products from the Loewy studio sold well. The combination of American production know-how and styling bravado allied to British craftsmanship proved to be a winner.

Scott is keen to scotch any notion that the Loewy outfit was concerned purely with style. He cites the street lighting that the team designed for GEC as evidence that the practice was as hot on production engineering as it was on styling. The street lamps were exported around the

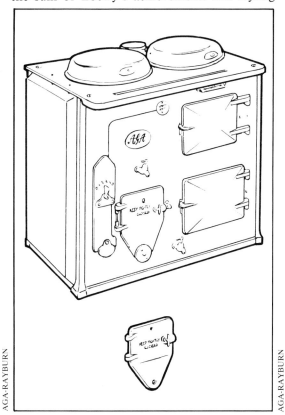

Drawing of Aga Solid Fuel cooker before Scott's redesign, 1934.

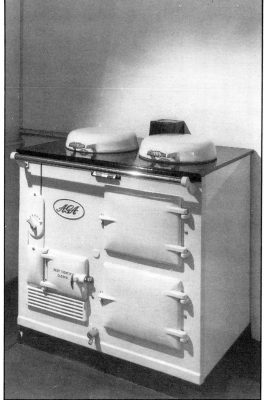

Scott's redesigned Aga Standard C cooker, 1938. Produced from 1941 until 1972.

world and are still in widespread use in Cyprus and Australia. The GEC commission was for a lamp which was easy to maintain. The Loewy team responded with a very simple hinged lamp cover, held in place by a quarter-inch section circular bronze toggle. It required the machining of very few parts which kept production costs well down, while in safety terms it was something of a breakthrough. Previous models required the man with the unenviable job of changing the light bulb to remove the cover using both hands while somehow clinging on to a ladder 20 feet up. Clearly four hands were necessary. The Loewy design reduced this to just two.

Theoretically at least, designs or blueprints were sent to Loewy for inspection, but this could delay small or urgent jobs as the blueprints took

Radiation cooker for John Wright, 1938. Designed for easy cleaning and to make full use of the latest techniques in preformed sheet steel panels.

Presentation watercolour of radiator heater showing influence of contemporary American car styling.

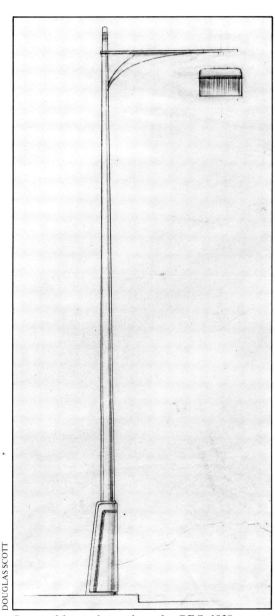

DOUGLAS SCOTT

Proposal for steel street lamp for GEC, 1938.

at least ten days to reach New York even by liner. Telephone calls were kept down to a minimum. Despite its glamorous image, the office worked to tight budgets. Scott found the office wasteful in one way though, and that was in Loewy's insistence that it produce a minimum of six variations on each project. It meant a lot of wasted drawings. Scott by temperament was anti-waste, particularly as the office produced well-finished tinted drawings. No wonder they were often up all night.

With Carl Otto increasingly out of the office touting for business, Scott found himself very much in charge on a day-to-day basis, and he was running the office by the spring of 1939. As the war loomed ever closer Loewy and Otto were in France and Sweden generating new business. Scott concentrated on product design, while Bill Snaith, an architect and later Loewy's partner, was responsible for the expanding interior design section. Snaith was a Beaux Arts educated American architect. Big, fat, explosive, he had bulging thyroid eyes, a girlfriend who had danced with the Ballet Joos, a good sense of humour and a brilliant line in interiors. He and Scott designed the memorable Lyons restaurant at 100 Oxford Street, famous for its infinity mirrors and the other tricks that became popular after the war. Snaith handled the interiors while Scott worked on the lighting.

The office at this time was working at its peak. The grey, white and blue décor was still smart, but the rooms in Aldwych House were crammed with bits of cars, trolleybuses, Raleigh bicycles, material samples for Commer commercial vehicles and lumps of brick, glass and plastic. Work for Rootes had expanded considerably, but Scott was never happy when the office was being pressed to design bits of cars. He spent what he describes as 'many miserable hours' working on dashboards, badges and rear-end light clusters. 'General Motors would even have

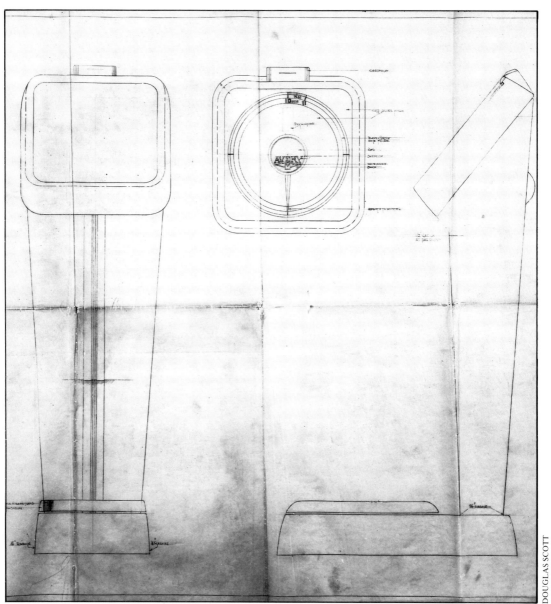

A common sight in post-war high streets: proposal for a coin-operated Avery weighing machine, 1939.

DOUGLAS SCOTT

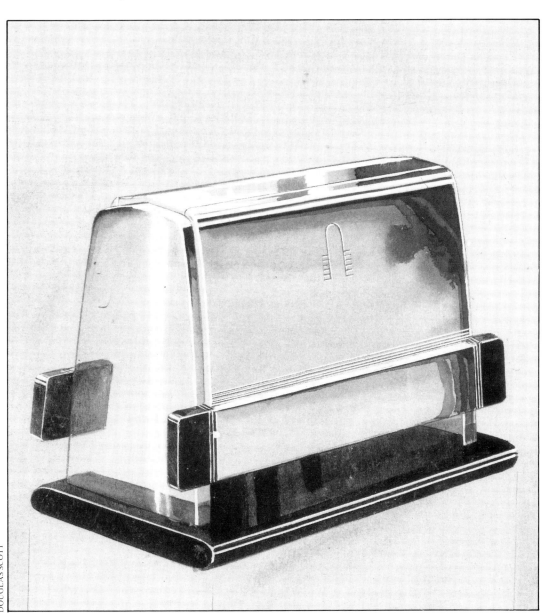

DOUGLAS SCOTT

Scott produced dozens of near-presentation watercolours for client approval. GEC toaster, 1938.

someone specialising in hub caps, but I always wanted to see a job through from the start to finish, and that meant thinking through the manufacturing process as well as the appearance of a thing.'

The chance to do just that seemed to come with the Hillman Minx project. The office mocked up three prototype cars at 1:8 scale. Each of these beautifully finished Plasticine styling exercises was given a different front-end treatment. The front ends were clearly Ameri-can-inspired, but not excessive. From the rear three-quarter view the car was decidedly British. There was clearly still more to be done with the design in terms of reconciling flamboyant American styling with conservative British engineering, but the war put a stop to further development. More than that, the declaration of war in September 1939 saw the end of the Loewy studio. The Americans working in the office packed their bags and went, soon followed by Carl Otto who was advised to return home. Scott

Hillman Minx mock-up in Plasticine at 1:8 scale, 1939.

DOUGLAS SCOTT

was given the business of closing down Britain's first fully fledged industrial design studio.

Drawings were packed and sent back to the Loewy office; Scott kept only those of his own designs. Loewy guarded his work jealously and no duplicate drawings were allowed to escape the net.

It is hardly surprising that Scott should look back on the Loewy days with great, if realistic, affection. At the age of 23 he was uprooted from the British craft tradition and transplanted into an American hothouse. His practical skills were never in doubt from his Central School days and these had been formed by the years with Osler and Faraday and GVD Illuminators. Working with Loewy, Otto, Beresford Evans and Snaith he now learned about style. In the post-war years he was to blend the two traditions and ways of working to produce thoroughly practical, yet inspired products. Working with Loewy had also introduced him to the great design debates raging in Europe and America. Scott joined the

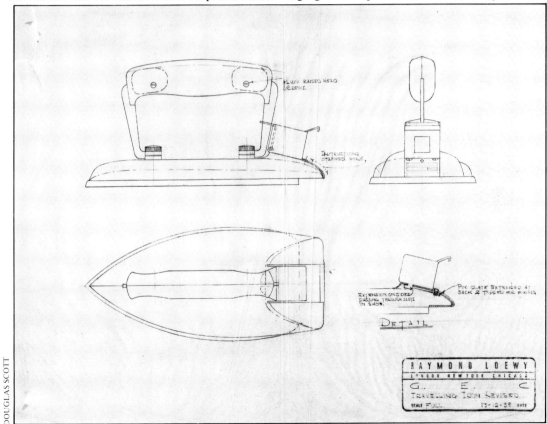

This travelling flat-iron was a straightforward, functional response to the GEC brief, without overt Loewy styling, 1938. Like all employees, Scott signed his drawings with Loewy's name.

DOUGLAS SCOTT

DOUGLAS SCOTT

Another commission for GEC, showing contemporary American influence. Coffee pot, 1939.

polemical Design and Industries Association (DIA) in 1939.

He was really sorry to lock up the office for the last time. 'We were just beginning to grow', he says, 'just beginning to make a real impact.' He could also claim many of the later jobs as his own: all the work for GEC and Electrolux, packaging for Harpers, a range of cast-iron household products, as well as design proposals for a new Rootes trolleybus and a three-wheeled Scammell tractor unit for Commer. He was also designing a tiny car for Rootes, a Hillman to rival the superb little Fiat Topolino of 1936. 'It was an animated bath chair', Scott recalls, 'I grouped all the controls around the steering column, which was something of a novelty then.'

Scott finally closed the door on the Loewy office in the first week of November 1939. It was a disorienting time. He had been in regular employment for ten years, had been earning a good salary and had recently married.

The first thing he tried to do was to get into the armed services. But it was the period of the 'Phoney War' and none of them would take him. Just before Christmas he took on a job at De Havilland, the aircraft makers, in Hendon not far from his Kingsbury home. The job was a temporary one as far as Scott was concerned, but it paid the bills and gave him a worthwhile wartime role.

Scott was to learn a considerable amount about production engineering and costing during his spell at De Havilland, but at first he was shocked by what he saw as lax attitudes and waste. Working flat out in the Loewy office for three years had not prepared him for the De Havilland accounts office. 'It was more one's idea of the civil service,' he remembers, 'it was all tea and chat and everyone knocked off at six o'clock. The whole accounting system was in a dreadful mess.'

Scott's energy and efficiency soon had him playing a larger role than De Havilland origi-

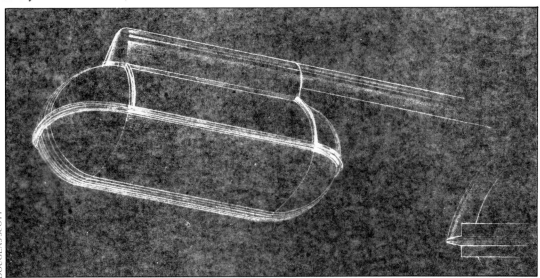

DOUGLAS SCOTT

Street lamp detail for presentation to GEC, 1938.

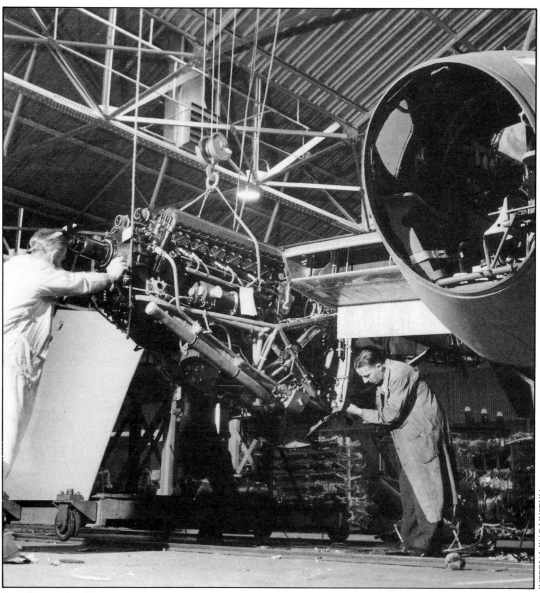

Installation of Rolls-Royce Merlin engine into a De Havilland Mosquito. Scott was involved in inspection and testing at the De Havilland plant.

nally intended. The company was still producing Gypsy Moth biplanes when he arrived, but experimental designs and development on the Rolls–Royce Merlin aero-engine were already under way. Scott found the accounts department boring. Major Halford's engine design department was recruiting staff and Scott managed to get transferred to the engine design department as a test assistant. He carried out various tests devised by the engineers. Slide-rules were used then – not calculators.

While this might seem odd work for a designer, it was invaluable experience for Scott. Later, after the war, the skills he learned at De Havilland – and the many that he taught himself – were put to use in such superbly efficient and reliable machines as the Routemaster bus for London Transport (1954).

In 1940 the newly formed Ministry of Aircraft Production directed De Havilland to build Rolls–Royce Merlin engines for use in Spitfire and Hurricane fighters. Scott became an inspector, first of engine parts, looking for crack damage and engine wear, and was then transferred to the assembly line, where his job was to examine the hand-assembled carburettors and superchargers. During the Battle of Britain in September 1940 he was soon working familiar hours, 12 hours a day, 13 days a fortnight, with a 4-hour firewatch each day either at home or at the factory.

A land-mine fell through the roof of the Scott home in Stroud Green and they went to stay with his wife's sister in Harringay. They had hardly settled in when during the blackout one evening Scott remembers saying 'that sounds just like an express train'.

The next moment the house collapsed: it had received a direct hit. The remarkable thing was that no-one was killed or even very seriously injured. Scott does not remember much. His head was injured and his shoulder blade broken.

He was taken to Muswell Hill hospital, but this was bombed during his three-day stay there. He and his wife Kathy took a brief holiday in Devon to recover. Bristol Temple Meads was ablaze when they steamed through. When they got back to Paddington a few days later the sirens were wailing. It was another raid.

Back at De Havilland, Scott learned a considerable amount about materials and component behaviour. With the Rolls–Royce-built Merlin he found some of the castings a little rough, yet because the alloys used were so good the engines were strong and reliable. The American Merlins built under licence by Packard and by Ford were superbly cast, but for some unknown reason they were down on horsepower compared with their British counterparts.

Scott teaching at the Central School of Art.

Chapter 3
Teaching Design

Almost without knowing it, at 32 Douglas Scott was one of the most experienced professional industrial designers in Britain. His craft background, his stylistic development at Loewy combined with his wartime experience on engines, materials, maintenance and costing all added up to a designer who really understood what made a successful product. Perhaps inevitably his wartime experience put him off style for style's sake, but although serious in intent and often sober to the point of being teetotal, his post-war consumer products – such as his low-cost washbasin for Ideal-Standard – have been some of the best-selling of all.

Scott could not abide waste or disorganisation. This was to make him a sound teacher, but also ensured that he would clash with the academic world which he first entered, again largely by accident, in 1945.

The accident was for Scott to become the founder of the industrial design course at the Central School, a department that Beresford Evans had tried to set up in 1939, when Henry Murphy was Principal. Misha Black also tried later in 1939, but the timing was not right. A R Emerson, Head of Metalwork, wanted to restart the department in 1945, and wanted Scott because he had had direct professional experience of industrial design and had a real grasp of materials and production methods.

Scott was still committed to De Havilland at the time, but began Britain's first product design course as a series of evening classes held from 6.00 to 9.30pm. Within this limited time-scale Scott set his first pupils – often fresh from the forces – jobs that they could execute at home. Scott himself was then working at home in Finchley using the attic room as his studio. He already had a small commission from St Andrews Mills designing a paper-towel dispenser and was also experimenting with designs for furniture made out of sheet metal.

But the teaching soon began to take up more of his time. There were 50 students in 1945. Scott recruited Ronald Ingles to assist him, but the two days he put in were gruelling – more 12-hour shifts. Those early students included Martin Rowlands, Desmond Sawyer, Doug Webb, George Collett and David Ogle.

The course was decidedly *ad hoc*, with Scott effectively making it up as he went along. His main concern was to show students how to get the best out of materials and to design up and down to a cost. Students were given a price which they had to work to. The first two projects were for the design of a kettle and a dustpan. These might sound prosaic but they enabled Scott to teach everything he knew about the commercial aspects of design along with techniques for die-casting, injection moulding and sandblasting.

While the new head of industrial design was improvising his course, the American magazine *Interiors* published an industrial design supplement complete with the curricula of the six leading design schools in the USA. Scott adopted the essentials of the American curricula, but as these were based on a five-year minimum course his own inevitably had to be less ambitious in scope.

Scott's course is remembered as a tough one. It was definitely not a fine art training, but a disciplined apprenticeship in practical, saleable product design. Scott's concern was to make the transition from college to the drawing office as painless as possible. He was very keen to demonstrate how restrictions in price or materials could be overcome. The course was based on simple familiar designs in a structured programme of materials, starting with sheet steel, then sandcasting, die-casting and plastics, eventually covering most of the materials and processes used by industry.

But this realism was seen by some in the academic world as too limiting. How could students be expected to produce new solutions to design problems if Scott kept hemming them in with fixed notional prices and materials? When Willie Johnson took over the Central School he attacked Scott for his obsession with cost. Scott was reported to Department of Education inspectors for 'restricting creativity'. Not unnaturally he resigned. He had spent four hard years getting Britain's first industrial design course off the ground. If it had little appeal for aesthetes and academics, then others could take it on. Besides, by now Scott had enough work of his own to set up in practice, which he did with Fred Ashford whom he had taken on before the war at Loewy's.

Scott was to teach again occasionally at the Central School, and years later was to set up another new industrial design school, but this time in Mexico where his matter-of-fact approach was greatly appreciated.

Scott's head of department at the Central School from 1945 was A R Emerson. This tea pot and cutlery set are examples of Emerson's work at the time.

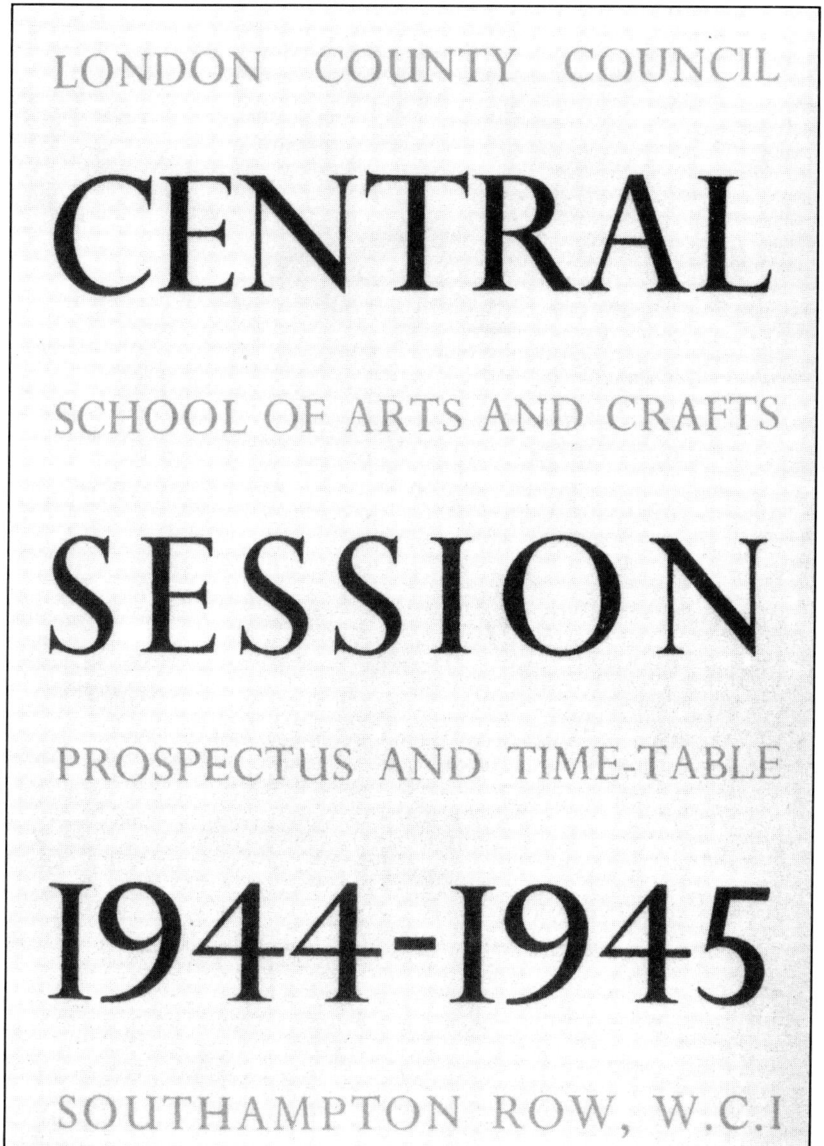

LONDON COUNTY COUNCIL

CENTRAL

SCHOOL OF ARTS AND CRAFTS

SESSION

PROSPECTUS AND TIME-TABLE

1944-1945

SOUTHAMPTON ROW, W.C.I

CENTRAL SCHOOL OF ART AND DESIGN LIBRARY

Scott began teaching his industrial design course at the Central School in 1945. This is how the course was announced to prospective students.

STUDIO FIVE/JOHN COLE

Fred Ashford, Scott's partner from 1949-53.

Chapter 4

Scott–Ashford Associates
1949–55

Fred Ashford and Douglas Scott set up in partnership in the basement of 100 Gloucester Place in 1949. They collaborated over the next four years, but Ashford's energies were drawn increasingly to teaching at the Royal College of Art and to sailing his boat off the Sussex coast. When the partnership folded in 1955, Scott took most of the clients with him.

After the war Scott could have taken on a new job with Raymond Loewy. Loewy and Carl Otto showed up at the Ritz soon after VJ Day. They were opening a new office in Grosvenor Square. Would Scott like to run it? He turned the offer down. The reasons he gave were that it would be too much work – Scott now had young children – and that, anyway, he wanted to flex his own muscle. But, more than that, Scott saw that Loewy was moving increasingly into packaging. It was not what he wanted to do. There were no

hard feelings and while Scott went his own way the Loewy office would feed him the occasional product development job.

Scott had just finished a freelance commission for a set of matching luggage for Papworth Industries in 1947 when he and Ashford began working together. The Papworth luggage is interesting for being the most overtly luxurious project Scott has ever worked on. The individual cases, presented to the ballet dancer Margot Fonteyn at the start of her tour of the United States in 1948, were beautifully detailed. In this design, as in any other, Scott was unable to work as a mere stylist. He learned from Thomas Lamb's studies in the USA to work on ergonomically correct handles and on other practical details such as the steel channels on to which the lids of the cases closed to ensure a smooth and reliable fit. The locks were gold-

DOUGLAS SCOTT

Set of luxury luggage for Papworth Industries, Cambridge, in tan leather with suede tops, tartan cotton lining and gold plated metalwork, presented to Margot Fonteyn, 1947.

plated, the leather a goldish tan and the interior trim a bright tartan – the Buchanan tartan, chosen by the works manager because it was easier and cheaper to obtain than the Hunting Fraser which Scott preferred.

Another major early job occured when Norbert Dutton, a typographic and packaging expert and a member of the Design Research Unit (DRU), contacted Scott some months before VJ day in 1945 at the Central School and after two or three meetings asked him if he would help out on a product they had contracted to design. It was a ship's binnacle for Henry Hughes and Sons.

Traditionally these bulky instruments, dominating the bridge of every ship, had been made of wood and brass. A shortage of materials in the immediate post-war years meant that the DRU were called in to redesign a binnacle in new materials. While the new instrument presaged a flow of work in tidying up old-fashioned, cluttered machinery and reworking old designs in new materials, it proved unpopular among old sea dogs. The company that had to install the new design found that nine out of ten skippers refused to accept it. They wanted the nautical equivalent of the wood-framed radio receiver. 'The new instruments had the same guts as the ones they were to replace', Scott recalls, 'but to the ships' crews they simply didn't look like a binnacle should.' The follow-up for Henry Hughes was a casing for their new echo-sounder, which looks ordinary enough now but was quite a radical departure at the time.

But Scott–Ashford's first job was considerably more low key and set the tone for the kind of work they were to specialise in. It was for a series of moulded plastic control switches for Proscon, the St Albans-based electronics firm. The central heating control is typical of the range – a simple grey plastic moulding set off with a maroon switch. In 1973 when Scott visited a Mexican colleague's house, the first thing he noticed was one of his own thermostat designs on the wall.

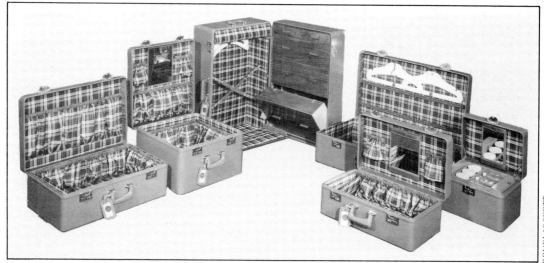

DOUGLAS SCOTT

The Papworth luggage set, showing the bright Buchanan tartan eventually selected for the lining.

This small commission led to a steady stream of work in the electronics industry. The very next job was a control desk for relayed radio broadcasts for Rediffusion together with a home receiver and a wall-mounted receiver switch. The contrast between the two types of product is a fascinating one. The studio control desk remains remarkably undated. The dials and switches follow a relentless, functional logic, while the sheet steel cabinet is simple and stream-lined. But the home receiver was finished in

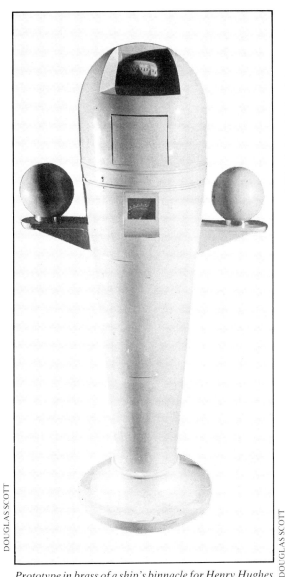

Prototype in brass of a ship's binnacle for Henry Hughes & Son Ltd, 1949. This design proved unpopular among ships' officers, who felt that it did not match their preconceived ideas of what a binnacle should look like.

From the late 1940s Scott began to design a vast array of control and switch gear. An early example is this moulded plastic thermostat control for Proscon.

materials that have definitely dated: wood-effect Bakelite for the casing and woven cotton for the speaker baffle. Why the yawning gap between these complementary pieces of equipment? The answer is simple. Scott believed in a straightforward appeal to the market. The receiver was designed to fit into the traditional dark polished wood interior of a typical English middle-class drawing-room of the period. It was also the case that until the transistor revolution, domestic electronic equipment was inevitably bulky, so radios and televisions were designed as pieces of crafted furniture rather than as dispensable accessories. Hidden away in a broadcasting station, the control unit could be as modern and functional as necessary.

Scott became interested in the presentation of control systems. The fault, as he saw it, in most contemporary instrument panels, switchgear and controls lay in their *ad hoc* design. Engineers would position switches and dials where appropriate for the workings of the machine, but, more often than not, would fail to think out the visual or ergonomic logic of what they were doing. If Scott can be accused of taking the romance out of Victorian control gear, the case for his defence lies in the fact that he made a considerable amount of machinery both safe and simple to use.

Scott's designs in this field give the impression of utter simplicity. Yet to rationalise control systems in the age of valves, oil-fed dials, cables

DOUGLAS SCOTT

Above: *Loudspeaker cabinet and programme selector switch for Rediffusion Ltd, 1946-7, making use of wood and fabric to soften the focus of new domestic technology. Programmes were broadcast to these sets using Scott's control desks* (right) *which, in contrast, show an uncompromised approach to design.*

and switches was no simple matter. In the 1980s sophisticated electronic and computer machinery can be housed in the most outlandish sculptural cases, or can be reduced to the tiniest packages, simply because designers no longer have to contend with the tortuous web of wires, valves and switches with which Scott was faced.

But rationalising the design of equipment did not mean reducing everything to straight lines. Above all Douglas Scott is a pragmatic designer responding to a brief rather than to a self-imposed aesthetic. The results were sometimes surprising. Take, for example, the battery testing unit he designed for J Langham Thompson for use by the British army in 1949. At first sight this piece of equipment abounds with curves and angles. Could this be a very early prototype for Ettore Sottsass's Memphis collection of the early 1980s? In reality, what look like superfluous curves and wilful angles are practical ways of making the machine work as logically and satisfactorily as possible. The display board is set at an angle to avoid the distracting reflection of light on the dials. The curves of the desk top are ergonomically considered elbow rests, while the drawers are designed to pivot without taking up a lot of space or thumping into the operator's leg. The design is a commonsensical exercise in functional logic which just happens to end up in a series of curved planes and angled surfaces. Had Scott been less pragmatic and more concerned,

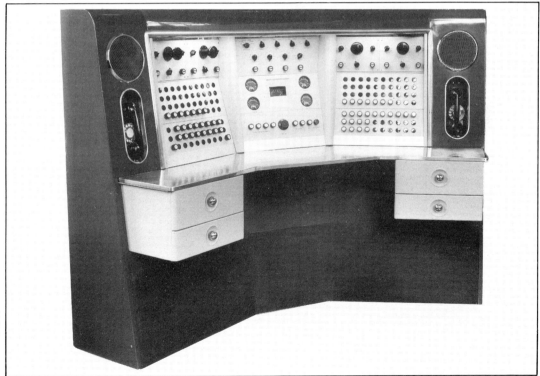

DOUGLAS SCOTT

Dry battery tester for use by the British Army. Designed in separate sections for speedy dismantling and re-erection. The design of the desk is not gratuitous; its quirky lines were shaped more by ergonomic than aesthetic considerations. Commissioned by J Langham-Thompson, 1949.

DOUGLAS SCOTT

as many designers and architects were at the time with a functional *aesthetic* rather than true functionalism, this battery testing unit would have ended up framed by a grid of right angles. It might have looked neater, but a generation of battery testers would have cursed both the machine and its designer.

It was about this time that Scott became involved with Milner Gray, Norbert Dutton and Misha Black of the Design Research Unit. Scott still sees them as highly successful public relations men with a lot of verve and style. Dutton and Gray were friendly with Mr Watney, a 6ft 7in (2m) giant – 'when he sat up he unfolded like one of those jointed steel rules' – who worked with WO Bentley, the designer of the original Bentley cars.

Dutton and Gray were keen to get a commission to design the new Lagonda Bentley was planning. As it turned out, Bentley only wanted a front end – the rest of the body would be fabricated from existing panels. Models were made the Loewy way; the DRU produced glamorous watercolours and Lesley Durbin the silversmith was commissioned to make a prototype radiator grille to Scott's design. But Bentley decided to remain true to more conservative designs. Scott felt the whole exercise to be a waste of time. He was far less interested in graphic styling exercises than in designing pragmatically from scratch.

His knowledge of production techniques came into its own when he was asked to design a range of very cheap wedding-gift clocks for Westclox. Muir Glenn, the Glasgow company's managing director, had searched in vain for a designer who could make a clock that buyers would be proud to give as a wedding present, but which would sell for as little as possible. Given the production price he was aiming at – seven shillings – Glenn could only really hope for a blatantly functional small steel-case clock. But what he wanted was a clock that would appeal to

low-income buyers in Scottish cities. Somehow the clock had to look grand. Glenn found Scott through the new Council of Industrial Design.

Scott's solution was one that set the style for a whole generation of low-cost suburban mantelpiece clocks. To keep costs down he suggested a full face in wood with the mechanism set in a cheap metal cylinder behind. Scott approached Design Furniture in Wandsworth who were then making Gordon Russell cabinets for Murphy radios. They suggested Scott use offcuts from the radio cabinet to form the clock front. These would cut very cheaply, as did the silk screened clock face Fred Ashford designed using gold leaf to pick out the raised figures. Silk screening alone reduced the cost of the face from Westclox's original estimate of 1/7d (8p) to 1/¼d — a penny farthing — no more than the cost of a silk screening impression using thick metallic type ink. These economies meant that the outer casing of the mechanism and the wooden face could be finished to a very high standard; in fact most of the seven shillings allowed by Westclox went into finishing the clocks. 'It was a quality job', says Scott, 'and nothing to be ashamed of.' The clock in two versions went on sale in 1953 at a price of 36 shillings (£1.80); it was a considerable success and its form was widely copied.

But Scott's most important client at this period was London Transport (LT). Through London Transport he was to design his masterpiece the Routemaster bus (see chapter 5). But the vehicle on which Scott began work was the intriguing RTC (Regent Type Coach), a luxury Green Line double deck coach based on London Transport's standard production RT bus (built 1939; 1946–54). Norbert Dutton and Ronald Ingles had originally produced a design for LT through an article in *Art and Industry*, but LT's decision to keep to the half-cab had caused problems with the front end which they called

Scott in to solve. Between 1946 and 1954 no less than 4825 RTs were built, a key part of Frank Pick's legacy of refined standardisation. But there was only one RTC. It was essentially a rolling laboratory of design ideas and was never intended for mass production. Yet it did give a number of clues as to the shape and characteristics of London Transport's next production double decker, the Routemaster.

The RT, designed in the late 1930s at London Transport's works, was a notably handsome bus. It was all of a piece visually and vastly superior to any other contemporary double decker. Such was the harmony of its sophisticated appearance that any change could only upset it.

The RT was a styling exercise, an attempt to streamline the established double decker idiom. Although Charles Holden, the architect of

Standard production RT bus (1946-54), precursor of the Routemaster. Designed by London Transport at Chiswick Works.

LONDON TRANSPORT MUSEUM

London Transport's stations and much of its corporate image under Frank Pick, had been invited to modify the bodywork of an LPTB double decker in 1931, this was the first time London Transport had approached an outside design consultant. The RT was the summation of 40 years of inspired engineering design, constantly updated and improved. Dutton and Ingles had given the prototype RTC a dra- matically angled front curving smoothly down from the roof to the bottom of the radiator grille. This made the double deck coach look sleeker and faster than the standard bus. Head- lamps, foglamps and registration plate were grouped together with a false radiator grille. The radiator – exposed on the production RT – was covered over with a curved panel (heralding the bonnet of the Routemaster) but the junctions of

Front-end view of Dutton & Ingles prototype RTC bus as remodelled by Douglas Scott for London Transport, 1946-7, based on the RT, opposite.

the half-cab wall, the engine cover and the radiator panel posed many problems for Scott to solve. He had to integrate the various elements that composed the front end of the bus. This streamlined effect was continued along the sides of the body with the sealed windows (the bus was equipped with forced-air ventilation). The light-coloured band running around the middle of the bus was a green acrylic panel – the legend 'Green Line' at front and back ends lit up at night.

The upper and lower saloons seated far fewer passengers than in a conventional RT. The tubular steel seats with integral handrails and footrests were provided with soft foam rubber cushions covered with a loose tartan moquette cover pattern design was by Ronald Ingles. In trials the seats proved too soft while the loose covers rucked up too easily, spoiling the effect. If not entirely to Scott's satisfaction, the RTC was nevertheless an important test bed for the Routemaster.

In 1948 Scott was commissioned to design the bodywork and interior of London Transport's new RF (Regal Four) coach. Three versions of this new bus based on AEC's new Regent IV chassis were required: a crew-operated bus, a Green Line coach and a private hire sightseeing coach. The first 25 private hire vehicles were worked on and ready for the opening of the Festival of Britain in 1951. (AEC was London

London Transport RF observation coach, designed by Douglas Scott and the LT team in 1948. The first 25 were produced for the Festival of Britain in 1951.

Green Line RF coach, showing fully integrated streamlined interior. Moquette design by R Ingles and N Dutton. Designed by Douglas Scott and the LT team in 1948.

RF Green Line coach, rear view. Here the windows are treated as a single unit.

Transport's subsidiary bus manufacturer based at Southall in Middlesex. Later hived off to British Leyland, it was eventually run down and ignominiously closed).

Scott's RF was a striking bus when it first went on the road. The vehicle appeared to have been extruded from one long piece of curved sheet steel. It was a streamlined vehicle almost completely free of appendages. The windows, a more or less continuous band of glazing, were set flush with the bodywork. Scott was keen to get away from the idea of windows punched like holes into the sides. He succeeded.

A full scale Plasticine-over-plywood mock-up was made at LT's Chiswick Works before work on the body began. Scott still likes the vehicle, but readily points out its two major flaws – one functional, the other aesthetic. The functional problem is the narrow entrance with its steep steps. The aesthetic problem is the way the big destination blind box sits in the high cornered front end. Scott would have preferred a more sloping front, but London Transport were insistent on a full destination display. But these are relatively minor niggles in an otherwise crisp design. The complex curved panels make the RF seem a much smaller vehicle than it really is – it looks a lot friendlier, for example, than the bulky Leyland National single deckers which replaced it in the 1970s. The bodywork abounds with neat details which help to maintain the effortless appearance. The radiator grille cap, for example, lurks behind a hinged LT bull's-eye motif at the front of the bus.

DOUGLAS SCOTT

Cantilevered canteen seating for LT bus garages. These were originally devised by LT's welfare office and redesigned by Douglas Scott with Roy Perkins c.1950. The first installation was in Clapham garage.

Full-scale plywood and Plasticine mock-up of AEC Regent lorry cab. Designed by Douglas Scott in 1953.

If the exterior is in any way compromised, the interior is a small masterpiece: fully integrated, beautifully made and minutely detailed. The sightseeing coaches were top-glazed, the glass screens curving round the sides of the smooth bodywork. These coaches were designed to carry visitors to and from the Festival of Britain and Scott was allowed to choose the livery. The buses were leaf green up to the roof line, grey-green above; hub caps and lettering were picked out in red. In all their 35 years on the London roads, the RFs never looked outmoded. Although styled in a new idiom they nevertheless blended in neatly with London Transport's powerful design tradition.

Working with London buses brought Scott-Ashford the job of designing canteen furniture for LT's bus garages. The brief said that the new furniture must be 'crew proof'. Bus garages are lively places and there is a long tradition of good-natured ribaldry; so chairs in particular suffer heavy wear and tear.

The LT Welfare Officer invented it and made a crude prototype which Scott-Ashford got into production form. The simple welded structure was immensely strong, while the cantilevered seats meant that chairs stayed where they were supposed to and sweeping the floors was made easier than it had ever been. Two prototypes were made in 1954. Both had cast-iron bases and heavy 16-gauge steel seats. Bus crews could lean against and swing on the seats without inflicting damage.

Scott had now been invited to work on the Routemaster bus. Shortly after the development of the prototype between 1952 and 1954, he split with Ashford. It was an acrimonious finish to what had been in many ways a successful partnership. But, true to form as a behind-the-scenes man, Scott was doing too much of the work. He set up DS Associates in 1955 at 100 Gloucester Place where he had been since 1948, and most of his clients stayed with him. Fred Ashford pursued a career in teaching and set up his own practice. Scott's practice developed rapidly with more architects and a variety of assignments.

LONDON TRANSPORT EXECUTIVE

Prototype Routemaster double deck bus for London Transport, 1953. Scott's original proposal was for a full-width cab, but LT senior management, engineers and unions demanded the half-cab treatment shown here. Without a radiator grille, RM1 was prone to overheating.

Chapter 5

The Routemaster Bus

The Routemaster (RM) bus is not just the most efficient and best-looking double deck bus to have run anywhere in the world, but a symbol of London and a paradigm of the best of British design. It is, in short, a masterpiece. Characteristically, Scott has never been able to see it that way. A man who has kept well away from the limelight, Scott's name has never been associated publicly with the bus that should have made him a household name.

For Londoners and tourists alike the Routemaster is *the* London bus. From the operators' point of view it has been a total success. There is still no satisfactory replacement for the RM. Unable to afford custom-designed buses for the 1990s, London Transport has brought to an end a century-long tradition of elegant, popular and reliable buses.

Built between 1959 and 1968, the capital cost of the buses was written off years ago. Under-

Early production RM, 1959. The bus was now fitted with a large radiator grille and modifications to the forced air ventilation system, which was to prove unsatisfactory during the summer. Buses of this vintage were still in regular service in 1988.

LONDON TRANSPORT EXECUTIVE/H ZINRAM

standably they were expensive to build, but given that the buses have been on the road for up to 30 years the investment has been more than worth it. The Routemaster, along with its predecessors, has been a key part of the London streetscape over the past 30 years. The new generation of buses bought off-the-peg from Leyland, Metro-Cammell-Weymann (MCW), and Scania are ugly, unloved, inefficient and noisy. Interiors of new one-man-operated double-deckers are illogically planned, while the detailing is crude. Colour schemes are execrable. The RM was the last bus custom-designed and custom-built by London Transport. The fact that these buses are rapidly disappearing from the streets of London (and are being snapped up second-hand by operators elsewhere in Britain) has nothing to do with their performance or longevity and everything to do with a mis-directed management policy.

The RM summarises Scott's approach to practical styling. In essence the standard bus is a large aluminium box measuring 27ft 6in by 8ft by 14ft 4in high (8.38m by 2.44m by 4.37m), seating 64 passengers. But the bulk of the vehicle is disguised by the subtle curvature of the body-work. Curves soften the focus: the RM seems much smaller than the ungainly red shoeboxes disfiguring London's streets today. Scott avoided the shoebox look by curving the base of the bus gently from above the rear destination blind box, rounding the rear side panels and curving the front sections of the bus in from the second window bay. Yet, despite its successful appearance, the bus is not quite as Scott would have liked it.

Scott was first approached to work on the RM in 1952. London Transport's engineers had started to think about a monocoque (chassis-less) construction. They wanted to reduce the

Standard production RM, 1960-6. Passenger comfort was improved by the addition of traditional quarter light wind-down windows on the top deck. A lengthened version of this model, the RML, was built between 1966 and 1968.

LONDON TRANSPORT EXECUTIVE/H ZINRAM

weight of a double decker by about a ton (the RT weighed 7.5 tons (7.6 tonnes) unladen) to save on fuel and wear and tear. They also wanted the bus to give the smoothest ride possible. Experimental engineering work had begun in 1951.

The engineers had come up with a monocoque aluminium construction supported by independent coil springs (some later buses were fitted with air suspension at the rear). But the shape of the new bus eluded Eric Ottoway, LT's Chief Engineer (Buses) and his widely experienced team at Chiswick. A long tradition of conservative engineering had culminated in the lovely RT bus of 1939. Scott was called in on the basis of his successful work with the RF single decker.

It was a prestigious commission. Scott worked with five LT engineers on the new bus. Restrictions on the design were tough. The bodywork had to conform to the exact dimensions laid down by the Metropolitan Police Carriage Office. There were to be no quirky details. The bus had to be simple to maintain and easy to clean. London buses were kept in immaculate condition until about 1970. Inspectors sited at garage exits were charged with sending dirty buses back to be cleaned before picking up passengers. The curved bodywork of the RM made for easy cleaning – surfaces flowed naturally into one another with no abrupt angles. To squeeze the maximum number of passengers into the given dimensions there could be no gentle fall-away slope at the front of the vehicle – as, for example, with the prototype RTC. To get any leeway and to avoid a tram-like or shoebox body, Scott felt he had to, in his words, 'steal the shape, pinching on half an inch here, three-quarters of an inch there'.

The first mock-up body had a full front, a radical change from the traditional half-cab. But there were protests from the Transport and General Workers' Union representatives. The drivers felt it would be harder to drive and that access to the engine would prove difficult. It was also felt that it was more considerate to front seat passengers to offer them an unhindered view out of the bus. The return to the half-cab approach gave Scott the problem of designing a satisfactory bonnet. Just when he felt he had achieved that, the AEC diesel engine was modified; the engine now projected slightly beyond the cab and the bonnet line had also to be raised to accommodate a new power-steering pump. Scott thinks that the projecting lip of the RM's bonnet is not quite right. He would have liked a further 3½in (9cm) of play to create a longer snout, but restrictions on dimensions were not to be gainsaid.

When the prototype RM was put on the road in 1954, senior LT staff still felt it looked too much like a trolleybus. This was certainly the view of the Chairman, Anthony Valentine. But what killed the flush-panelled front end was less to do with appearances and more to do with keeping the engine cool. The forced-air ventilation system was also to prove unsatisfactory and wind-down quarter-lights were added to the front of the top saloon in later production vehicles. LT management were disappointed that the bus, weighing in at 6.75 tons (6.86 tonnes), was 56lb (25.4kg) heavier than the contemporary mass-produced Leyland Tiger despite persistent attempts to shed weight. The production RM was a little heavier at 7.25 tons (7.36 tonnes). Scott calculated the weight of the scarlet paintwork and suggested that 3 cwt (152.4kg) could be saved if the bus was finished in bare aluminium. It was an interesting experiment, but the 'Silver Routemaster' drew howls of protest from outraged Londoners. It was duly painted red.

The interiors had to be the best possible. Initially Scott wanted fibreglass frames for the seats, but these proved heavier than traditional tubular steel and plywood. He also looked at fluorescent lights which would have been fitted in panels flush with the ceiling, but the initial cost was excessive and anyway it was much easier for garage staff to replace traditional screw-in tungsten bulbs (these are also kinder to the worn faces of commuters). The rear platform was to have been covered in a rubber composition but on test this proved inferior to maple wood, which LT has always used in its tube trains. The new tartan moquette seat fabric designed by Scott proved very durable and is still used. Primrose yellow paintwork above the

windows not only made the RM interior seem sunnier than earlier vehicles, but was also Scott's way of combating nicotine stains.

Numerous minor changes were made to the production buses, particularly in the treatment of the grille and front wings, but basically the production buses followed Scott's design.

Scott's contractual position with London Transport was a curious one. Never officially contracted to work on the design he was paid small fees in fits and starts. In fact he made very little money out of his most famous design. 'I

enjoyed the job so much that I didn't really think of the cash.' It was a very personal service Scott gave London Transport and, although financially he benefited very little, he gained an immense amount from the experience of working with such highly skilled engineers and production teams.

The next London bus should have been a development of the Routemaster. Although London Transport engineers were working on a new vehicle, political circumstances put an end to the project. London Transport began buying unsatisfactory off-the-peg buses from British Leyland in 1970. More than fifteen years on from the Routemaster the new buses weighed in at 10 tons (10.2 tonnes), featured a massive antique chassis, leaf-spring suspension and, in effect, zero design input. In a misguided publicity campaign London Transport labelled the Leyland bus 'The Londoner'; it was something of an insult to passengers and LT engineers to say the very least.

In another country Scott's would have been a household name for the design of the Routemaster alone. But he has never really understood why his name should be celebrated. For a professional designer, it was just another job.

LONDON TRANSPORT MUSEUM

Interior shots of RML double deck, upper deck (above) *and lower deck* (left). *The RML was a lengthened version of the standard Routemaster.*

DS ASSOCIATES LTD/BANKS TURNER ASSOCIATES

DSA offices at Tileman House, Upper Richmond Road, Putney – more of a research laboratory than a conventional design studio. Scott is seen (right) examining full-scale models of the Ideal-Standard Roma WC pedestals.

Chapter 6

Douglas Scott Associates

Douglas Scott is a retiring man by nature. He is not attracted to bright lights or glamour. Unlike his contemporaries Misha Black and Milner Gray he chose to stay in the background. It seems appropriate that most of his work has been to do with the silent servants of the product world – the kind of materials that we need and use daily but rarely think about: slide viewers, tin-openers, stamp machines, control gear, sprinklers and vehicle testing equipment. But because he has naturally avoided working with expendable fashion-led consumer goods, his work has endured.

By the early 1950s Scott's career was largely set. He was a designer of hard-wearing, easy-to-maintain equipment that was simple to operate and good-looking in a straightforward way. Never a slave to fashion, many of the products he designed are still in daily use or still in production 20 or 30 years after they were first designed. The London Fire Brigade still use Douglas Scott-designed fire engines (the AEC Regent, first mocked up in Plasticine in 1953 and bearing a family resemblance to the Routemaster bus); his GPO telephone pay-boxes have only just been phased out; Routemaster buses still outperform the latest generation of London double deckers in terms of speed, economy, comfort and reliability; his street lamps illuminate the highways and byways of Sydney; his wash-basins for Ideal Standard are ubiquitous.

Scott has never been a self-conscious artist.

DS ASSOCIATES LTD/L G AUBIN

Reel-to-reel tape recorder for British Sound Recorders. This unit was designed to fit into any number of different cabinets manufactured worldwide. Designed by Douglas Scott, 1957.

His concerns are to do with economy of materials, ease of maintenance and ergonomics married to a handsome is as handsome does aesthetic. It is almost by accident that his work is sometimes beautiful rather than simply handsome or easy on the eye. No one was more surprised than Scott that his Ideal Standard wash-basin should have been given a permanent space in New York's Museum of Modern Art. The lovely line of this product came about for purely functional and practical reasons (see chapter 7).

But, if he avoided the limelight, Scott was never short of work. Glamorous jobs occasionally came his way through long-term clients and Scott had several of these, a number of them stretching from the early days until 1976 when he ceased his full-time practice and went to teach in Mexico (see chapter 8).

One of these was Dr MacDonald, Chairman of British Sound Recorders (BSR) for whom Scott designed both a record deck and a tape deck. The BSR tape deck sold world-wide in hundreds of thousands. It was designed to be as

DS ASSOCIATES LTD/BEKEN OF COWES

simple as possible. The design had to be very restrained as the BSR equipment was sold to other manufacturers for inclusion in their own equipment. Finished in two-tone grey with gilded lettering it was exactly right for the world market in 1957. On the proceeds of his profits, MacDonald bought the hull of a motor yacht from a boat yard in Poole in 1957. He asked Scott to design the superstructure and the interiors after he had rejected a number of architects' drawings.

MY *Tamarind* was launched in 1958. Scott

kept the superstructure low giving the boat a long, sleek line. *Tamarind* was a fast boat and she looked it. The cabins appeared positively luxurious given Scott's propensity for a certain starkness of finish. The colours were rich – deep blues, reds and purples; the panelling was in exotic veneers.

Partly on the strength of *Tamarind*, Scott was asked to design the superstructure of the Halmatic Ocean 25, a popular glass fibre reinforced boat, largely maintenance-free and designed for fast cruising. Its twin 110hp Volvo Penta power

PACKAGE DESIGN ASSOCIATES

Left: *MY* Tamarind *on sea trials, 1957. The superstructure, including the state rooms and crew's quarters, was designed by Douglas Scott and Peter Casson.*

Above: *Dining room of MY* Tamarind. *Scott seldom used such rich finishes as the walnut veneer lining the walls and cabinets.*

units and twin drives pushed it up to speeds of 40 knots, fast for 1963.

But the bulk of Scott's work from 1953 to 1976 was for a relatively small number of companies who stuck with him for years. One of these was Donald Paterson, a Scottish dentist, barrister and keen amateur photographer. From very small beginnings Paterson achieved a good reputation during the 1950s as a manufacturer of high quality slide viewing, storage and projection equipment. It was a very specialised market but one that grew rapidly as the quality of colour transparency film improved. The first design in 1952 was for an injection-moulded pocket slide viewer. It was a very simple instrument that looked good and fitted neatly into the hand.

One of the most intriguing pieces designed for Paterson was a collapsible viewer for 2¼in (5.7cm) square transparencies. Made from four intersecting injection-moulded polystyrene components, the viewer, when flat, folded neatly into a tiny powder compact-like box

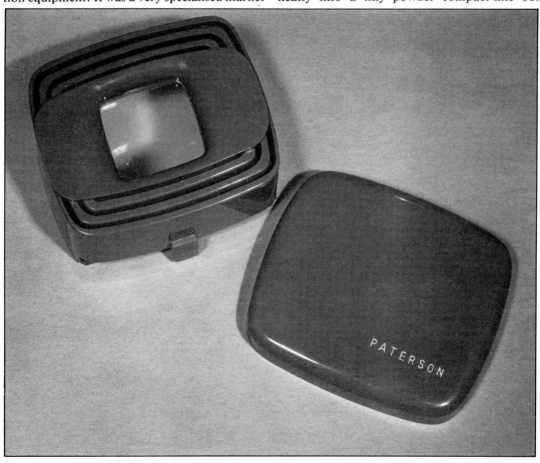

which could be carried in any pocket. Extended, the viewer had the look of a small green armadillo. It is now something of a collector's item.

Other equipment for Paterson included a dark-room safelight, a contact printer with a translucent yellow plastic body, a 150W slide projector, plastic processing beakers, a pistol handgrip for cameras and some smart injection-moulded plastic slide boxes. These were designed to stack on top of each other and are still to be found in photographic laboratories.

Mass transparency storage has been achieved with the '200' series of slide boxes, which are designed to stack in such areas as institutional archives.

English Electric (EE) had been producing a powerful AC electric motor for years, mostly for use in mines. When the motor was given a new core, Scott was asked to redesign its casing. His solution won favour with English Electric not just on the merits of its clean, modern image which made it easier to sell, but because Scott

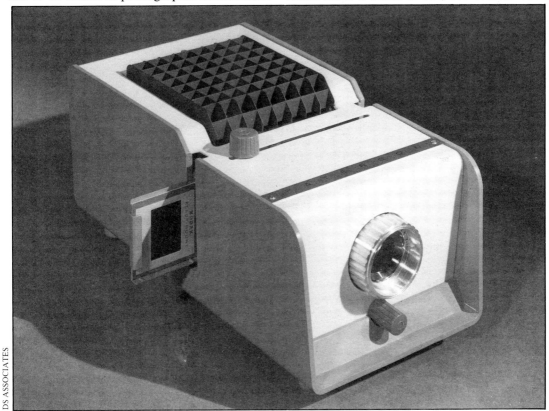

Left: *Pocket-sized collapsible viewer for 2½inch transparencies for Paterson Products, designed in the early 1960s, and produced in green polystyrene.*
Above: *A 35mm slide projector with egg-crate cooling panel for Paterson Products, 1960.*

DS ASSOCIATES

looked at the motor as a whole and could see a way to reduce machining time and so reduce production costs. The core of the improved motor was held in a welded ¼ in (6.5mm) plate-steel cradle with removable panels bolted on. The product now required no casting, fewer components, weighed less and was cheaper to make; a workaday commission and unlikely to hit the pages of a fashion magazine.

Through their successful work with Marconi, a sister company, Scott's team was asked to work on a new computer for English Electric, who felt they had a good product, but the various pieces of equipment looked a mess. In 1968, Stanley Kubrick's '2001: A Space Odyssey' was about to create a love affair between a wide public and the computer. EE had to be up to the minute. The problem was easily solved. Each piece of equipment in System Four was related, but each had been produced by a different team of engineers. The result was therefore visually illiterate. Scott framed the various pieces of equipment in a related sequence of neat cabinets which gave System Four an integrated and purposeful look.

Shell, another company concerned with

DS ASSOCIATES

In 1965 Scott was asked to rehouse one of English Electric's powerful electric motors (above). The new cladding was designed to allow easy cleaning and transport, the motors stacking neatly together in transit (right).

presenting its public with a white hot, technological image, wanted a blend of functional good looks, common sense and prestige for its new building control centre in the basement of the recently completed Shell Centre designed by Sir Howard Robertson on London's South Bank. The problem here was very similar to that of the English Electric commission. Control over the heating, ventilation, lighting and security of this vast building complex was concentrated in one underground centre. The labyrinth of equipment in the basement was baffling. Scott's job was to devise a systematic way of displaying the controls and ordering the dials and switches. Scott designed a 52ft (15.85m) sequence of identical aluminium panels to force order from the chaos. That, plus clear logical graphics, meant that the state of the building's control systems could be seen at a glance. The intriguing thing about this job is to see just how many old-fashioned controls were used in the new panels. When it opened in 1962, the Shell Building control centre was a Boys' Own adventure playground. Distinguished visitors were ritually brought underground to gaze at dials and watch men in white coats press switches and shift levers.

Other jobs for Shell proved too sophisticated to be practical on a day-to-day basis. One was for the design of a prototype Speedline servicing

unit for garages (1963); another the design of a self-service petrol station (1969). Both projects were just ahead of their time.

The Speedline car servicing unit, which promised to save motorists and garages hours of wasted labour, was probably too sophisticated,

Magnetic tape unit for English Electric System 4 computer, 1967. The prototype System 4 units were a random collection of mismatched cabinets. The designer's task was to make the individual units visually and functionally compatible. Douglas Scott and W Rossi Ashton.

too space-consuming and too expensive a piece of equipment for most garages even to contemplate buying.

The majority of cars required servicing every 1000 miles (1600km) in the early 1960s; some had recommended service levels as low as 500 miles (800km). This meant that average motorists needed their car servicing every month. Shell's idea was that they could sit in a waiting-room sipping a hot drink from a vending machine (prestigious in 1963), while watching task panels light up as each job was done on their car. The cars meanwhile were treated to a rigorous testing process. Six cars could be serviced at any one time and no pit was required.

The self-service project was an expensive and rather sad folly. Scott was brought in to design it and approached the architect Boyd Auger to work on the steel roof, designed to cope with heavy snow loads. Scott and Auger hit on a triangular plan for the petrol stations, the idea being that cars would no longer get stuck behind each other as they did in conventional service stations. The model alone cost £1500 to make, but Shell dropped the project less on cost grounds and more because it was felt that British motorists would never want to have to serve themselves. A month after the project was dropped, Scott recalls, the first self-service petrol station opened in London.

Scott won his first Council of Industrial Design Award in 1963 for the STD telephone coin-box and the second in 1967 for the Hy-Mac excavator for Peter Hamilton Equipment Ltd. The latter was another Scott redesign, an area in which he had become expert. Although a sophisticated and reliable piece of earth-moving machinery, it was a new venture by the company in a highly competitive field with well-established products. Peter Hamilton wanted to ensure a strong position in the market and put their faith in industrial design. In retrospect it is

DS ASSOCIATES/BANKS TURNER ASSOCIATES

DS ASSOCIATES/JOHN MALTBY LTD

Above: *Car servicing unit for Shell, 1962. The idea was to speed up the process at a time when the average family car required attention every 3,000 miles, and to offer the motorist a while-you-wait service. Designed by Douglas Scott and W Rossi Ashton. The lightweight structure was the work of the architect Boyd Auger.*

Below: *Proposal for 9-pump self service station for Shell, 1967. The roofs were designed to cope with heavy snowfall. Designed by Douglas Scott, with Boyd Auger as structural consultant.*

easy to see why. The Hy-Mac 480 was a jumble of bits tacked together which appeared to bear no relation to one another. Scott was told in all sincerity that 'excavators aren't bought on appearances', but guessed, rightly, that was patently untrue.

Scott's job was simple and satisfactory. Applying Loewy principles he repackaged the machine. It was transformed almost overnight from a rough-and-ready looking piece of agricultural equipment into the kind of exciting giant toy that all grown-up boys want to play with and sales soared. Scott worked with Bill Rossi-Ashton on this task. They modestly said that it was simply a question of 'tidying things up'. But some fundamental changes were made to the equipment. The big diesel engine was laid down on its side and covered with sheet metal.

In 1965 Scott was asked to redesign the clumsy Hy-Mac excavator imported from US by Peter Hamilton Ltd (left). *The Scott version* (above) *boosted sales through a combination of greater stability, all-round visibility for the operator, easier access to the engine and control equipment, and good looks.*

This gave the excavator a lower, broader look, which appeared, and was, more stable and efficient than it had been before. Tools could be stored under cover on the platform instead of in the cab, which itself was designed to a standard that construction workers had never previously enjoyed in Britain. The Hy-Mac range was later extended to wheeled as well as tracked vehicles.

Although Scott was very busy in the 1960s, the financial ups and downs of working as a designer encouraged him to join forces in 1962 with James Pilditch. They set up the bigger group Allied Industrial Designers and took offices first in Clifford Street and then in Rathbone Place. But the alliance was not as successful as Scott had hoped and he withdrew his team in 1970 to continue under his own steam.

The next few years were spent largely with major clients – Marconi, Associated Automation, Prestige and Ideal-Standard. But throughout the 1960s Scott had been designing for a variety of small companies. It is worth looking at some of these before examining his major development work for large corporations.

One of the most curious Scott designs is a lightweight folding caravan dating from 1963. The Farlander was designed for a private client and built by Comptons the organ builders. The aim was to produce a cheap caravan that could be towed safely by the average small car normally too low on horsepower to pull a substantial trailer. The brief was also for a caravan that could be erected very quickly. At the 1963 Earls Court Motor Show a 10-year-old child erected the caravan in just 70 seconds.

The caravan was made of lightweight fibreglass honeycomb panels. It weighed 8 cwt (406kg) and because the suspension was well thought out it could be towed rapidly. Much lower and more compact than a conventional caravan it was less affected by cross-winds on exposed or fast roads. When folded for towing, the caravan resembled the back end of a contemporary Ford Consul or Austin Cambridge. But there was a functional purpose behind the design of the ribbed boot structure and the vestigial fins. The ribs strengthened the back wall of the caravan when erect, while the sloping back of the trailer afforded drivers the best possible rear view.

DOUGLAS SCOTT/UNIVERSAL LENS CRAFT

Farlander caravan for a private client, built by Compton Co, the well-known organ builders. Designed by Douglas Scott and Roy Ireland, 1963. The style of the trailer complemented contemporary car design. When towed, the sloping top panel offered drivers good rear visibility. When opened (left), the caravan offered four-berth accommodation. The end wall could be raised, as shown, in good weather. Sadly, the craft skills needed to make the Farlander proved too costly, and production was limited.

Four-ton dockside crane for N C K-Rapier, Ipswich. W Rossi Ashton and Douglas Scott.

The Farlander was a fine example of how to squeeze a quart into a pint pot, but it was never a success. For the caravan to work properly the standard of workmanship had to be very high. That was hardly a problem for Compton whose craftsmen were highly skilled. Yet it proved problematic because the amount of skilled labour that went into making the Farlander pushed the cost too high. But it was a brave attempt and one still worthy of fresh appraisal.

In contrast a small mobile crane for Ransom Rapier was an immediate commercial success. Like the Hy-Mac it was one of those vehicles that looked fun to use, a full-size Tonka Toy, and so attractive to both buyers and users. In British Rail's black and yellow livery it looked like a busy bee as it was buzzing around railway dockyards.

While these projects were being tackled, Scott was also producing an analogue computer and aircraft seats for Short Brothers, electrical control gear for use in developing countries for Johnson and Phillips, car-tuning analysis equipment for Crypton, an exhibition display system for Tube Investments, ships' compasses for Stanley Investments and a document transmitter for Sendox.

All these smaller projects show Scott's tidy mind at work. The trailing wires of the Crypton equipment, for example, were neatly stowed in sheet steel boxes. Grey sheet steel was very much Scott's stock-in-trade. Although a very unfashionable view in the 1980s, Scott believes that many of the objects we use should be efficient, silent servants. We want a ship's compass to tell us the direction in which we are sailing; we want instruments to be as clear and as logical as possible, particularly when they control complex programmes or concern our safety. Scott's designs of the 1960s were logical, hygienic and relentlessly concerned with efficient production engineering. When fashion

swings against over-indulgent, over-expensive design in the next few years Scott's calm approach to machinery will be appreciated again. Scott has never expected anyone to get excited about some of his designs. They are meant to be functional tools yet styled with sufficient flair to make people want to buy them rather than a rival product.

Scott's only venture into the world of direct retailing came with a commission to design supermarkets for Galbraiths – 'the Sainsburys of the Clyde Valley', as he described the group. Several stores were built between 1967 and 1970. Scott enjoyed the challenge to begin with, 'but after the first three it got a bit boring'.

The store at Cumbernauld, the brutal 1960s New Town, is typical of the Galbraith shops. The shop is very large and well equipped, yet its design and layout follow a rather cold and inexorable logic. Supermarket chains are

Aircraft seating for Short Bros, Belfast, 1967.

Crypton fault diagnostic unit for testing engine performance. Previously this type of equipment comprised a potentially dangerous tangle of wires and meters. W Rossi Ashton and Douglas Scott, 1965.

notably keen on uniform lighting levels aimed at speeding customers through the stores. Yet Scott's false ceiling system went some way to baffling the glare of fluorescence. His shop within a shop approach was also novel for the time. Although a little dry, the Galbraith store took the design of supermarkets a neat step forward to the cosseting 'village street within a brick shed' style of the 1980s.

A look at Scott's own offices at the time of the Galbraith commission gives some idea of his clear functional approach to design. More of a research laboratory than an artist's studio, the Putney practice was housed in a modern office block. It consisted of a large open-plan space subdivided where necessary by lightweight, glazed aluminium panels. The lighting was uniform, the floors covered in hard-wearing white linoleum, the walls white, and daylight filtered through grey aluminium blinds. To Scott the way a product performs and endures is as important as the way it looks. Small wonder that his office would have more appeal today to engineers and computer scientists than to fashionable designers.

BRYAN & SHEAR

Interior of Galbraith supermarket, Cumbernauld New Town, 1967. The fluorescent lighting was designed to be free from glare. The diamond shadow effect was fortuitous but unintended. This was Scott's only venture in retail design. Douglas Scott and R Hidden.

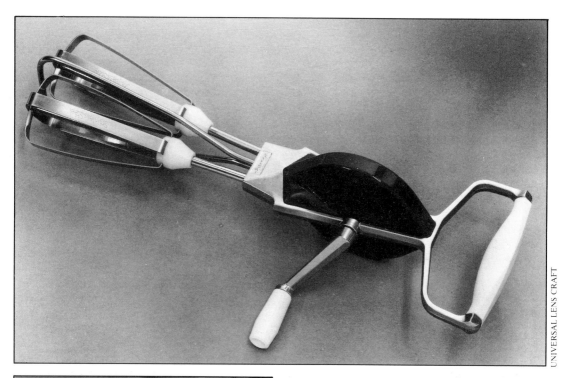

UNIVERSAL LENS CRAFT

JOHN MALTBY LTD

Above: *Redesign of traditional hand whisk for Prestige. Colour was introduced for the casing to move the product up-market. Douglas Scott and W Rossi Ashton, 1967.*
Left: *Icing gun for Prestige Group. Douglas Scott, 1967.*

Right: *Low-cost Roma washbasin for Ideal-Standard, Italy. The shallow, non-British Standard, shape of the basin was determined by the continued habit of washing babies in the sink and by the production firing process which caused cracks and thus wastage in more complex forms. The Roma washbasin has a permanent home in houses throughout the world as well in the Museum of Modern Art, New York. Designed in the early 1960s by Douglas Scott.*

Chapter 7
Major Clients

Douglas Scott believes that one of the major failings of British industry in the immediate post-war era was its refusal to invest in new tools and equipment. Whereas many European and Japanese companies were forced to make a clean break, British industry picked up the threads from 1939. At a time when any consumer good could be sold there seemed to be nothing wrong with this head in the sand approach to industrial production. But when the consumer boom took off in the mid-1950s, the British public were able to choose the goods they bought and suddenly home-produced goods began to pale in contrast with those from West Germany and Japan. 'Buy British' campaigns could not halt a decline brought about by industry's refusal to learn new tricks after the war.

When Scott began working with Prestige, the American kitchen and bathroom equipment manufacturers, he found its British subsidiary reluctant to invest in the new tooling he recommended. A designer's job, he was told, was to add style and catch the consumer's eye. Scott felt otherwise and said as much. When planning

long production runs, a designer should design new tools, working alongside production engineers. When pre-orders for some of Scott's designs could total up to £4 million, it seemed churlish to hold back funds for investment on the factory floor. Scott's approach may have seemed an extreme one to manufacturers looking for product changes every year, but Scott has long held that the right product, well thought out and well made, can stay in profitable production for many years. His work for Prestige and Ideal-Standard was soon to bear this out.

Scott's other great design alongside the Routemaster bus is the low-cost Roma washbasin for Ideal-Standard. In production since 1964, this basin is no less elegant and satisfying for appearing in millions of houses throughout the world. It also has a secure place in the collection of the Museum of Modern Art in New York. If Scott had worked on a royalty basis with Ideal-Standard he would be a wealthy man. True to character he produced a masterpiece on a shoestring and for a small design fee.

This job came to Scott, who had already been

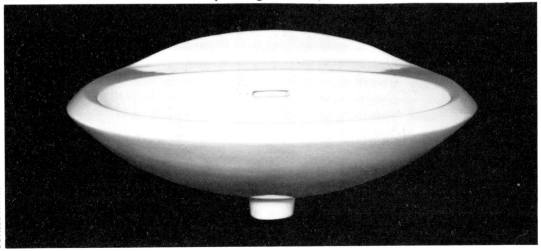

DS ASSOCIATES

working on the design of domestic boilers for Ideal-Standard in Europe, after it had been turned down by the Milanese architect and designer Gio Ponti. Ponti felt that Ideal-Standard were looking for a Ferrari on a Fiat budget. Scott saw no difficulty. A good product can be produced on any budget as long as that budget is fixed in the designer's and manufacturer's minds from the inception of a new project. Scott felt that Ponti may not have wanted to be associated with the cheapest wash-basin Ideal-Standard had ever considered making.

How did Scott produce such elegance at such low cost? The answer was in his careful research into the properties of the raw material for the basin: vitreous china. Scott discovered that the failure rate of Ideal-Standard basins under firing could be high, so he began looking for a shape that would fire evenly and easily with little prospect of failure in the oven.

The full scale mock-ups, however, were made in plaster of Paris. The shallow, scalloped shape Scott revealed was an optimum trade-off between satisfactory firing and the use to which the basin would be put in the majority of households. So the shape was also determined by the manner in which European mothers bathed their babies at the bathroom sink. A third important factor determining the shape was the need to stack as many basins as possible on one trailer to reduce transport costs.

Scott remains stoical about design awards and accolades. 'You don't set out to make a classic when you're designing', he says, 'you just get on with the job in hand.' Perhaps the most delightful aspect of this basin (complemented by a handsome WC pedestal and bath) is that it gave low-income families a higher standard of design than wealthy middle-class householders who, needing to buy 'up-market' bathroom fittings,

Wash-down Roma WC pedestal, designed for easy cleaning and low-cost production.

Rondamatic domestic boiler for Ideal-Standard, 1967. This hygienic design replaced traditional horseshoe boilers. Douglas Scott and E Cordell, 1967.

had to choose less well thought out and less elegant products. This pleased Scott, a socialist before the war and no élitist after.

Scott had long been interested in ergonomics and one of the jobs that came his way through Ideal-Standard was the design of a three-piece bathroom suite for the 1967 Ideal Home Exhibition at Earls Court. The big name in bathroom design at the time was Alexander Kira, a professor of ergonomics, commissioned by the US government to write an official report on the state of bathroom equipment. The Kira report turned orthodox attitudes to bathroom design on their head. Kira proclaimed a new approach to the design of bathroom equipment.

The bathroom, he said, was not just a machine for cleaning people, but more a way of life. Contemporary lavatories were not designed for the human form. They encouraged constipation and ultimately bowel cancer. Bath fittings were designed to make life easy for plumbers and uncomfortable, even dangerous for the bather. The British Medical Association came down heavily in favour of the Kira Report and Ideal-Standard was quick to respond.

But the ensuing prototypes for the post-Kira bathroom were very hurried. 'We were meeting exhibition deadlines rather than human or production needs', Scott recalls. 'It was a bit of a stunt when you look back.' The only properly

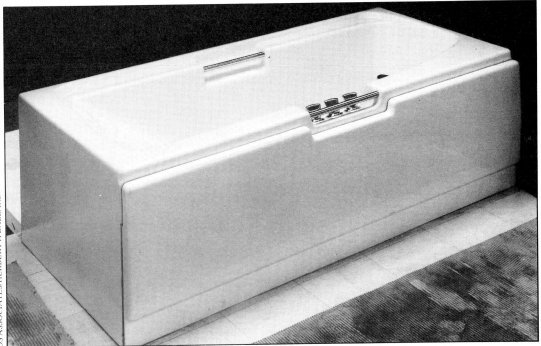

DS ASSOCIATES/HERBERT H BALLARD

Acrylic bath from Ideal-Standard's ergonomic bathroom suite, produced for the 1967 Earls Court Ideal Home Exhibition. The taps were placed within easy reach of the bather and grab handles were provided for safety. Designed by Douglas Scott and John Cooper.

finished product was the bath Scott designed. Made from vacuum-formed acrylic plastic and designed according to ergonomic principles, it incorporated grab handles and taps mounted low on the side which could be reached from a sitting or lying position. But although these features have been taken up since, production costs looked prohibitive at the time. The acrylic technique alone cost £90 when the average price of a standard vitreous enamel bath was £25.

Scott also mocked up a domestic urinal, which nobody seemed to approve of at the Ideal Home Exhibition, and drew up plans for a low level WC pedestal. Although attractive in principle, Ideal-Standard baulked at the cost of developing an appropriate and effective flushing mechanism and the project was quietly dropped.

Aside from baths and basins, Scott was also designing a range of domestic boilers for Ideal-Standard. Perhaps the most significant, in Britain at least, was the Super Rondamaster which was designed as a replacement for the venerable horseshoe boiler which, dating back to the nineteenth century, was still being fitted to local authority houses in the 1950s. Although the horseshoe boiler might have a certain charm now, residents of 20 and 30 years ago associated it with the worst aspects of Victorian Britain. In kitchens blessed with new cream and, increasingly, white cookers and even refrigerators, the cast-iron horseshoe boiler seemed unhygienic and out of place. A boiler which provided a family that had 'never had it so good' in the late 1950s with hot water and heating from behind a smooth white casing was a blessing in sheet steel.

Cleanliness is a major concern in Scott's work. Those old enough to remember London, for example, before the Clean Air Act of 1956 will recall how dirty the atmosphere was: the airborne dirt was clearly visible. People wanted their homes to be clean, even if their collars and cuffs were coated in fine layers of soot within

minutes of leaving the front door. Perhaps the cult of sanitisation went too far, but at the time Scott was designing exactly the right products for the market.

From the early 1960s Scott did a lot of work for the GPO through Associated Automation, makers of telephones and other standard equipment for this major client. Some of the designs Scott produced have stood the test of time; others have been made redundant because of rapid changes in telecommunications technology.

At the time the GPO was keen to rationalise (a buzz word of the 1960s) the eclectic accretion of machines and equipment it had inherited during the century. One of the first jobs offered to Scott was the design of a new standard Post Office clock. In fact he designed two, both a familiar sight in the high streets of Britain.

The difference between the two versions lay in the clock faces. One used simple marks for

GENERAL POST OFFICE

the hours and minutes, the other Arabic numerals. Otherwise they shared the same Associated Automation hands, mechanism and casing which was produced in diameters of 9, 12, 18 and 24 inches (22.9, 30.5, 45.8 and 71cm).

At the same time Scott expended a considerable amount of effort on the design of new stamp-issuing machines. Some of these were designed to be free-standing in high streets to cut down queues inside Post Offices. As vandalism and street crime increased in the 1970s and 80s, so these red and black machines gradually disappeared.

More important and longer lasting than Scott's stamp-issuing machines was his design for a new pay-box telephone. The old black and white public pay-phone with its famous Button A and Button B was a handsome design, but ponderous in operation. It was easily vandalised and often over-generous to generations of schoolchildren and tramps, who, trying their

GENERAL POST OFFICE

Left and above: *Standard clocks for GPO made in four sizes – 9, 12, 18 and 24 inches diameter. Designed by Douglas Scott in the 1960s.*

luck with Button B, would often hit the jackpot when a clatter of old pennies would come tumbling down into the refund tray.

Scott's new universal pay-phone was designed to fit into the existing K2 and K6 model telephone kiosks. Demolished for some unknown and perverse reason on an increasing scale by the privatised British Telecom in the 1980s, these elegant classical kiosks designed by the architect Sir Giles Gilbert Scott in the 1920s and 30s were still considered an essential part of the British street scene in the 1960s. Scott certainly thought so, although he did enter a competition for the design of a new pay-phone to complement his namesake's classic design. In any event, there was no need to alter the Gilbert Scott kiosks. The new phones, single pieces of equipment, fitted neatly into place. They were simple, robust machines that lasted until the arrival of a new generation of liquid crystal display pay-phones in the 1980s.

Scott's longest association with any one company was with Marconi. This fruitful relationship lasted from 1954 until GEC closed the company down in 1986. Marconi was a successful professional manufacturer of broadcasting equipment. But a take-over by GEC in the mid-1970s led to a painful decline.

Marconi was another client to whom Scott was introduced by the Council of Industrial Design (now the Design Council). The first job he did for the company was the design of a portable field telephone for use in the tropics. A sturdy machine, it has long been discontinued but remains very much in use. This was followed by versions of transmitting equipment for use by the Army.

But, aside from a vast amount of auxiliary electronic equipment, they were approached by the broadcasting division to work on TV cameras. They found the team of engineers led by Norman Parker-Smith quite brilliant and

IDCF/AD PHOTOGRAPHY LTD

L G AUBIN

Above: *Public telephone area in Heathrow Airport. STD machines designed by Douglas Scott and Peter Casson with Associated Automatic engineer Andrew Young in 1962. Scott and Casson also designed the directory holders.*
Below: *Portable vending unit for the GPO for use in exhibition halls and temporary buildings. It dismantled easily for transportation. Douglas Scott, 1964.*

good people to work with. The most important work Scott did for Marconi was the development of a new generation of their television cameras, starting with the Marconi Mk V of 1962. This camera began its days for use with turret lenses, but was revolutionised when the spider's eyes accretion of lenses was replaced by a single, all-purpose zoom lens in 1965. The prototype had to be ready within three months.

Prototype GPO public telephone kiosk designed for rapid manufacture and easy construction. The kiosks were low cost and simple to erect with minimum labour. Designed by Douglas Scott and W Rossi Ashton.

Under considerable pressure, Scott stuck diligently to Marconi's tough timetable and the result was an instant technical and marketing success.

Rather pessimistically, Marconi had only tooled up for the production of 50 Mk V cameras and had to revise its plans quickly: the camera sold in large numbers world wide for several years. Its appearance was radical at the time. The complex, bitty form of a conventional TV camera gave way to a compact box comprising three powerfully modelled elements: the viewer, the camera and the zoom lens.

Over the next four years several modifications were made to the original design. The Mk VI was designed for use in low light levels and the Mk VII was a small colour camera for which the timing of its introduction was critical. The camera was designed to coincide with the launch of colour broadcasting and had Marconi launched it too early, it would have been in danger of becoming prematurely obsolescent; had it been held back too long, Marconi could have missed the market. As it turned out the timing was perfect. The new camera, with a family resemblance to the Mk V, sold well. It won a Council of Industrial Design Award in 1967, while Marconi went on to win the Queen's Award for Industry the following year.

The Mk VIII camera followed in 1970. Powerful and compact, this new generation camera featured a miniature built-in computer which controlled picture alignment and colour balance at the touch of a button. Although a technical success, the camera did have its critics. The TV presenter Judith Chalmers was one who found the high speed zooming motion of the camera's lens as worrying as a victim facing Ridley Scott's 'Alien'. This problem was resolved and the camera continued in many guises, all designed by Scott, until the Mk XIII of 1986.

Almost as light relief, Scott designed a mobile outside broadcasting unit for Marconi in 1966. Based on a standard Bedford coach chassis, the unit had to meet a broad specification. The air-conditioned interior had to be as compact and lightweight as possible, while the exterior had to be glamorous, a mobile representative of television broadcasting. Bowling along the road, the big Bedford had something of the look of a modern gypsy caravan, glistening with polished chrome, light reflecting off the high-waisted, ribbed aluminum panels. The big low-cut cab windows helped make it easy to drive.

Scott's association with Prestige was not quite as long as with Ideal Standard or Marconi, but it did span the 15 years from 1961 to 1976. An American company based in Chicago, Prestige had a British subsidiary which, during the late 1960s and early 1970s, threatened to overtake its parent. The work for Prestige intrigued Scott. Small and wide ranging, Prestige equipment for kitchens and bathrooms had to be instantly attractive to buyers, but sturdy and long lasting. Starting with a set of bathroom scales, Scott pushed on through a plethora of wall-mounted tin-openers, vegetable slicers, knife sharpeners, icing guns, whisks, a coffee pot, a whistling kettle and carpet-sweepers. These were all simple designs, many a reworking of earlier products and just as durable as Scott's London buses.

Above: *Mk V TV studio camera for Marconi, 1965.*
Below: *Mk VIII colour TV camera for Marconi, 1967.*

MARCONI (GEC)

Outside broadcast mobile television studio on a Bedford chassis for Marconi, 1966. Marconi wanted a vehicle that was both functional and glamorous. W Rossi Ashton and Douglas Scott.

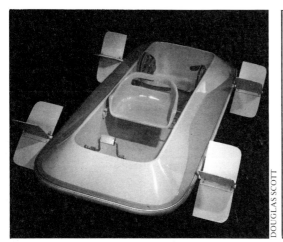

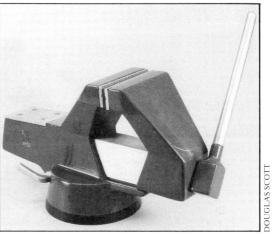

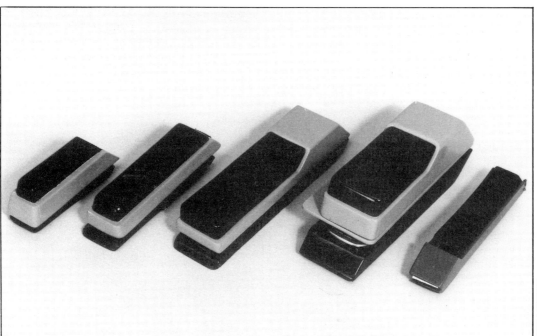

Work produced by Scott's first students in Mexico. The brief in all cases was to produce elegant products at minimum cost and using immediately available materials.

Chapter 8
Mexico

In 1966 Ramon Torres, Head of Architecture at the Universidad Nacional Autonoma de Mexico, came to visit Scott in London. He had already toured the United States, Germany, Italy and France. His goal was to study ways of setting up an industrial design course (the first) in Mexico. Ideally what Torres wanted was a package he could take back with him. Most of the courses he inspected in Europe and the USA he found far too theoretical. Mexico had pressing design needs and Mexican students, he believed, needed a shot of common sense.

In Britain he looked at design schools in Edinburgh and Glasgow, but left unimpressed. At the Royal College of Art Misha Black's course unfortunately did not strike the right note with him, so he tried the Central School of Art. Here he found just the kind of teaching he was looking for. The course was practical and Scott was still teaching there.

Torres returned to Mexico and attempted a Central School style industrial course from 1968. But he had serious misgivings. Taught by architects who, as Torres says, 'were much keener on monuments than on consumer satisfaction', and despite the best intentions, the course was at best another form of fine art training. Mexican manufacturers were not impressed.

Through contacts at the Central School, Torres invited Scott to Mexico in 1970 as visiting professor. Scott went and much to his own surprise fell in love with the country. Were it not for commitments at home he would have liked to settle there. But the 1970 visit was just for the duration of a summer school. Scott set his students practical tasks and was much admired by fellow teachers and pupils alike. Scott was invited back to run summer schools again in 1973 and 1975. Finally in 1976 he took the plunge and accepted a full-time job as Professor of Industrial Design, shutting up shop at Douglas Scott Associates after 40 years as a full-time practising designer.

Scott stayed for three particularly happy years. But the first few months were tough and somewhat frustrating. There was, he recalls, no sense of reality about the place. The students were undisciplined and were not used to working on real projects. Early results were poor. Scott instituted a tough regime: doors in the department were closed to latecomers at 9.30 am, conversations, which had often drowned out the teacher, were banned and students were discouraged from inviting family, relatives and friends to classrooms to continue heated arguments.

On a creative level, Scott gave short, illustrated lectures and set demanding but realistic project work. He maintained what he has always held, 'you can't teach good design, but you can teach an attitude of mind that leads students to producing good design'.

Douglas Scott receiving his second international design award, presented by the Japan Design Foundation in Osaka in October 1985.

Chapter 9
An Appreciation

Douglas Scott returned from a three-year teaching spell for family reasons in 1979. Photographs and articles in Mexican magazines stand as testimony to the no-nonsense approach he encouraged in those nine academic terms. If the projects he set were unglamorous, they introduced a large number of would-be Mexican designers to the realities, potentialities and limitations of factory production. Scott was teaching them to walk before they ran. In many ways this is exactly what he had taught himself over the years. Through a craftsman's training at the Central School, to perfecting design and manufacturing skills, Scott was always keen to master the processes that led him, unselfconsciously, to become an accomplished designer.

Even though he has hidden from the bright lights, Scott's achievement has been recognised by the professionals if not by a wider public. With numerous Design Council Awards to his credit, Douglas Scott is also a Royal Designer for Industry (RDI, 1974). In Mexico he was awarded the Mexican Institute's Gold Medal for Design in 1973 and ten years later the Society of Industrial Artists and Designers' Design Medal. In October 1985 he gained his second international design award, presented by the Japan Design Foundation in Osaka. Despite an attempt to retire after his stint in Mexico, Scott is still busy working as a design consultant for a number of companies keen to employ a designer with a real grasp of materials and production processes.

Scott is no propagandist, no polemicist. He has sought no acclaim and has made little money from his half-century as an industrial designer. He has, as he says, always been too busy to think about the money or any possible fame. Yet his best designs rank among the British classics. But in this respect Scott is no different from the dozens of backroom engineers and draughtsmen who produced some of the most elegant British machines and products of this century. If history were written by Douglas Scott he would have no place in it. Fortunately, despite himself, his major contribution to design cannot go unrecognised.

MODERN EUROPEAN DESIGNERS
A biographical record of 20th century designers

Other titles in this series:

	Price
MISHA BLACK By Avril Blake	£7.50
MILNER GRAY BY Avril Blake	£8.50
ALEC ISSIGONIS By Andrew Nahum	£8.95
HARRY PEACH Dryad and the DIA By Pat Kirkham	£9.50
ERNEST RACE By Hazel Conway	£6.50
ETTORE SOTTSASS JNR By Penny Sparke	£6.50
MARIANNE STRAUB By Mary Schoeser	£8.95

Copies are available from all good bookshops, or by post (add £1.50 post and packing per title) from

Design Centre Bookshop,
28 Haymarket, London SW1Y 4SU.